WIT

NCTE's Theory and Research into Practice (TRIP) series presents ...
of works designed to offer a teacher audience a solid theoretical foundation in a given subject area within English language arts, exposure to the
pertinent research in that area, and a number of practice-oriented models designed to stimulate theory-based application in the reader's own
classroom.

Volumes in the Series

*Co-Authoring in the Classroom: Creating an Environment for Effective
Collaboration* (1997), Helen Dale

Beyond the "SP" Label: Improving the Spelling of Learning Disabled Writers
(1992), Patricia J. McAlexander, Ann B. Dobie, and Noel Gregg

Illumination Rounds: Teaching the Literature of the Vietnam War (1992),
Larry R. Johannessen

Enhancing Aesthetic Reading and Response (1991), Philip M. Anderson
and Gregory Rubano

Expressions: Multiple Intelligences in the English Class (1991), Peter
Smagorinsky

Unlocking Shakespeare's Language: Help for the Teacher and Student (1988),
Randal Robinson

Explorations: Introductory Activities for Literature and Composition, 7–12
(1987), Peter Smagorinsky, Tom McCann, and Stephen Kern

Writing about Literature (1984), Elizabeth Kahn, Carolyn Calhoun
Walter, and Larry R. Johannessen

Questioning: A Path to Critical Thinking (1983), Leila Christenbury and
Patricia P. Kelly

Designing and Sequencing Prewriting Activities (1982), Larry R.
Johannessen, Elizabeth A. Kahn, and Carolyn Calhoun Walter

Learning to Spell (1981), Richard E. Hodges

Computers in the Writing Classroom

Dave Moeller
William S. Hart Union High School District

National Council of Teachers of English
1111 W. Kenyon Road, Urbana, Illinois 61801-1096

Staff Editor: Bonny Graham

Interior Design: Doug Burnett

Cover Design: Joellen Bryant

NCTE Stock Number: 08288-3050

It is the policy of NCTE in its journals and other publications to provide a forum for the open discussion of ideas concerning the content and the teaching of English and the language arts. Publicity accorded to any particular point of view does not imply endorsement by the Executive Committee, the Board of Directors, or the membership at large, except in announcements of policy, where such endorsement is clearly specified.

Library of Congress Cataloging-in-Publication Data

Moeller, Dave.
    Computers in the writing classroom / Dave Moeller.
        p. cm. — (Theory and research into practice)
Includes bibliographical references. (p.   ).
    ISBN 0-8141-0828-8 (pbk.)
  1. English language—Composition and exercises—Study and teaching (Secondary)
2. English language—Composition and exercises—Computer-assisted instruction.
3. Constructivism (Education) I. Title. II. Theory & research into practice.
    LB1631 .M513 2002
    808' .042'0285—dc21

                                                    2002001121

Contents

Introduction

To trace the early history of computer-assisted writing instruction, one need not go back very far—the early eighties will suffice. At that time, the focus of early theorists and practitioners was "elaborate software" (Rodrigues and Rodrigues 14); "word processing and document design" (DeWitt 71); "skill-and-drill tools emphasizing correct structures, sentence-level accuracy, and the communication of already known truths" (Takayoshi 254); and "drill and practice exercises, rote learning, grammar exercises, and spell checking" (Gruber 27). Today, however, the focus of research and practice is "network-supported writing facilities, collaborative writing, the political implications of electronic writing instruction" (DeWitt 72) and "the writing process, online conferencing, websearches, and webpage development" (Gruber 27). Clearly, there has been a shift in the way we view computers. Dawn Rodrigues and Raymond Rodrigues describe this shift as a move "from supplemental to integrative" (14). Underlying this early supplemental view of computers was the belief "that computer programs can replace teachers in their ability to handle certain subtasks of teaching" (15).

In the early days of computer-assisted writing instruction, it was believed that the best way to replace the teacher was through programmed instruction. William Wresch's 1984 compilation *The Computer in Composition Instruction* provides a sampling of the prevailing literature of this early period. Approximately half of this book advises teachers how to use programmed software such as SEEN, HOMER, COMP-LAB, WANDAH, and Wordsworth II. Included in these programs are grammar drills, instruction or tutorial in composition, and actual word-processing programs, offered singly or intertwined. Today such programs have all but disappeared from the composition classroom.

As teachers, each of us has his or her own peculiar attitude toward computers. Some of us might love computers; some of us might hate them. My own attitude is ambivalent. On the one hand, I hold to the tenets of the Luddites. Much is wrong in our world today, and I believe that much of the blame for our present ills can be laid at the feet of technology. I'm uneasy about the sudden and unquestioned omnipresence of computers in our schools and classrooms. Frequently, when I ask the question, "How have these computers improved the education of my students?" the answer is that they have not. Despite the grandiose claims by computer enthusiasts that computers are the panacea for our educational troubles, computers are used mostly for mindless entertainment and escapism. I am troubled by the ease with which we assume that computers are supplying us with immeasurable sources of learning, while in reality they are often stealing our precious time. And in my own classroom practice, I find that of the ideas and skills I've been teaching for nineteen years, none can be taught more effectively in a computer environment. With one exception: the skill of writing.

When I first began writing on a computer, it was as if I had entered a world of fresh and novel possibilities. Behold, all things had become new! I fell instantly in love with word processing and—despite my Luddite tendencies—couldn't imagine going back to composing by hand.

Once my own love for word processing had solidified, I wanted to share my enthusiasm with my students. I wanted to teach my students not just *writing,* but *writing with a computer.* For several years now, much of my teaching energy has been spent trying to bring the skill of and appreciation for writing with computers to my students.

The goal of this book is to present a reasoned, balanced approach to using computers in the writing classroom. The pitfalls of the computer are presented along with its advantages. As teachers, it is our responsibility to consider both sides of the issue and to make our pedagogical decisions in light of what we know. By studying both the pros and the cons of the computer, we are more likely to use computers wisely, and to use them only in those situations in which they are likely to improve the education of our students. Ultimately, I believe that the computer has one best use, and that use is writing. I also believe that the concept of the computer as primarily a tool of writing is an idea we should disseminate throughout the educational environment.

Theory and Research

1 Theory

This chapter moves from a discussion of current theory in the field of computer-assisted writing instruction to a discussion of constructivism—the dominant instructional theory that serves as the umbrella under which most other current theories and practices flourish.

Current Theory: Constructivism

The common element linking the various strands of current research and theory in the field of computer-assisted writing instruction is change—change brought about by introducing the computer into the composition classroom, or maybe, more specifically, the change brought about by the supplanting of pen and paper with the computer. Pamela Takayoshi notes four such change-oriented branches of study: "changes in writing processes of invention, drafting, and revision; an increased connectivity between students and teachers that brings with it an expanding exposure to different world views; an increase in multiple literacy demands on students; and fundamental changes in writing and reading processes" (245).

Like Takayoshi, Martha C. Pennington notes the changes in composition theory ushered in by the introduction of computers in writing classrooms. She characterizes the theory shift as a movement "from a surface level to a deep level of usage and from a separated orientation to an integrated orientation of usage" (63). This paradigm shift has in turn brought us to see the computer-as-writing-aid with new perspective. Pennington has devised the following chart to describe the computer as it was viewed in the early stages of theory and as it is viewed today (66):

Property	Early-Stage Model	Late-Stage Model
Status	Machine	Medium
Function	Fixer	Facilitator
Sensory Feedback	Stimulus to Writing	Stimulus to Thought
Workspace	Notepad	Exploratory Environment
Typing Capability	Typewriter	Text Generator
Mechanical Assistant	Transcriber	Creative Tool
Local Text Changes	Error-Corrector	Editing Aid
Block Text Changes	Organization Aid	Revision Aid
Saving Files	Final Text Storage	Current Text Storage
Printing Files	Task Completion	Redrafting Aid

During the early period of computer-assisted writing instruction, teachers made the mistake of putting new wine into old bottles; that is, we were trying to force technology into the preexisting instructional systems. The result is described in column 2 of Pennington's chart. As M. D. Roblyer points out, we were asking the wrong questions. We wanted answers to questions such as "Is computer-based instruction as effective as teacher-delivered instruction?" and "Will the use of word processing improve the quality or quantity of students' writing?" (12). Today we are moving away from the "achievement-boosting" questions of the past and asking questions such as "How can teachers use a given technology-based method to make collaborative learning possible?" and "What is the impact of using a given technology resource on the way a classroom functions?" (Roblyer 12). Our shift in the questions we now ask reveals once again a paradigmatic shift—away from what might be called "traditional" instruction and toward what is commonly known as "constructivism." Constructivism puts the experiences of the student at the center of instruction, and those who see constructivism and technology as symbiotic would argue that technology helps to "validate and share those experiences" (Kalmbach 65).

In most current theory, computer-assisted writing instruction and constructivism are wedded in inseparable bliss. Though from the far rearward reaches of the church a few faint voices might be heard to offer objections to this marriage of technology and theory, the mainstream consensus is to bless the newlyweds wholeheartedly. So let's get to know this kin-by-marriage. Practitioners of constructivism believe that "learning is . . . a personal, reflective, and transformative process where ideas, experiences, and points of view are integrated and something new is created—a view where teacher work is construed as facilitating individuals' abilities to construct knowledge" (Sandholtz, Ringstaff, and Dwyer 12). Put simply, the focus of the classroom is no longer the *instruction* delivered by the teacher to the students, but the *construction* of knowledge manufactured by the cooperative effort of the class—students and teacher together.

The Politics of Constructivism

Any instructor who adopts a constructivist stance is siding with democratic ideals over authoritarian principles, with romanticism over classicism, with the common person over the wielders of power and authority, with child-centered instructional approaches over teacher-centered approaches. Constructivism stands against "treating authors as a special category of human being"; instead, a constructivist teacher offers students "a chance to express their ideas and observations in powerful new ways" (Halio 348). Lisa Gerrard defines constructivism as "espousing collaboration" (25) as opposed to the "solitary writer" (26); advocating "students' power over their writing . . . and confidence in their own authority and experience" (26) against "drill-and-skill software that stifles students' ideas and implies that they are flawed and need correction" (27); and promoting "nonauthoritarian pedagogy," "the decentralized classroom," "an egalitarian pedagogy," and "democracy, pluralism, and cooperation" (27).[1] These are the political ideals an instructor linking composition with technology might aspire to. But political ideals, as instructional paradigms, are meaningless without the classroom practices to turn the theory into reality. In the case of constructivism, the operative words are *student centered*, *collaborative*, *groups*, and *peer response*, each of which warrants a closer study.

Student Centered

The move from a teacher-centered to a student-centered classroom demands that the instructor adopt a shift in paradigm. Debbie J. Williams sees this shift as "a transformation in the way power is (not) constructed in the classroom between teacher and student" (42). Williams describes the student-centered classroom as a place where "students are involved in more than listening" and where "less emphasis is placed on transmitting information and more on developing students' skills" (42).

That the student-centered classroom stands in contrast to the teacher-centered classroom might seem obvious; what might not seem so obvious is that the student-centered classroom also stands in contrast to the canon itself. According to Sally Tweddle and Phil Moore, the problem with the old paradigm was that instructors used canon-accepted authors as models, models that were "remote and abstract" (286). The average student can never hope to write like the great-and-powerful canon writer and therefore has "no likelihood of real success" (286). Tweddle and Moore's conclusion is that in our attempt to form a model of what the ideal instructional technology (IT) classroom should look like, "a canon of literature . . . cannot form the model's core. Rather, the model should place at its heart the notion of understanding, interpreting, and evaluating a writer's choices" (290–91).[2]

Collaborative

"Democratizing education" (Peckham 327) is one reason to have students work collaboratively on their writing. Another reason is that collaborative writing mirrors many of the writing tasks we now perform: "Important documents are drafted by committee and so also are less weighty pieces of writing. Letters and memos . . . [and] even fiction [have] been constructed collaboratively with electronic mail as the medium. No longer can one assume that an authorial voice is that of an individual" (Tweddle and Moore 283). Yet another reason to have students write collaboratively is that "group work especially enables students who are not naturally gifted academic high achievers . . . to understand and strengthen their lecture, discussion, and textbook lessons on writing" (Jewell 53).

Richard Jewell notes that teachers, when first faced with converting from a traditional classroom arrangement to a computer lab, often assume that their collaborative practices must be abandoned. Such an assumption, however, is false. Jewell's experience "has been that group work and any kind of computer lab can be married happily to teach writing" (52–53).

Groups, Peer Response, and Physical Arrangement

The classroom format that best accommodates constructivist practices is small groups. In addition to facilitating collaborative writing, small groups offer these advantages: students "work in closer proximity to each other, share each other's rough drafts, take responsibility in helping each other, look into each other's eyes, [and] cue to conscious and unconscious body language" (Jewell 58). The small group arrangement also allows the instructor to employ peer response methodology, which in turn provides advantages of its own. Chief among these advantages are the "sense of audience" that response groups provide, the facilitation of writers becoming readers who "*hear* their texts" and who "hear how others hear their texts," and the relocating of the editorial onus away from the teacher and onto the student writer (Peckham 328–29).

Once we have decided to adopt the principles of constructivism, with its concomitant commitment to small groups and collaboration, it then becomes necessary to arrange the physical structure of our classrooms accordingly. To begin with, straight rows, which are unable to accommodate groups, must be done away with. Richard Jewell suggests that "pods or clusters, circles, and perimeter designs" (54) take the place of straight rows. And beyond the attempt to hit on the optimum group-enhancing seating arrangement, the introduction of computers adds a new element to the equation: in the straight row model, the teacher must be in the front of the room so that he or she can see the students' faces; in the technology classroom, the teacher still benefits from seeing the students' faces but now must stand behind the students in order to see the computer monitors (Jewell 57). Furthermore, the concept of being in the front of the room is made instantly invalid—the front of the room no longer exists (Rodrigues and Rodrigues 21). Finally, the teacher who endeavors to arrange the classroom so as to best accommodate small groups and peer review will discover that the level of noise and chaos is greater than it was in the straight row days (Sandholtz, Ringstaff, and Dwyer 21). Many teachers find this early transition period a disturbing and disquieting one.

Structuring Small Group Instruction

Irvin Peckham lists five requirements for successful peer response groups:

- Response groups have to mesh with the larger classroom strategy of collaborative activities.
- Papers need multiple readers (a minimum of three).
- Respondents generally need reasonably concrete criteria or notions of what to look for.
- Respondents need a strong sense of a full rhetorical situation so that they can respond from the situation's perspective.
- It helps (a lot) if the essays are on subjects that interest both writers and readers. (329)

Richard Jewell also suggests groups of three, with the further stipulation that each group member be given one of three roles: "coordinator, writer, or reader" (55). Sibylle Gruber suggests that "computer experts" be "grouped with those less comfortable with the technology" (29).

Once the groups are formed, the next step is to provide students with guidelines for commenting on student papers and for marking them with editorial comments. Rick Monroe has adopted the techniques of the oral, pen-and-paper read-around groups and modified them to suit computer composition. Instead of distributing paper, he passes out disks. He still uses the oral components of the read-around—pointing (echoing back), active listening (saying back), center of gravity (discovering the heart of a piece of writing), believing and doubting (from Peter Elbow), lurkings (what is *almost* heard), and suggestions (for making the piece more audience-friendly) (8–10). But instead of using these response techniques as they were originally envisioned, Monroe's students use them to respond to peer writing by typing responses directly onto the original text.

Dawn Rodrigues and Raymond Rodrigues have noted that students are more willing to make comments on computer-generated texts than on handwritten papers. Students know that their comments on computer-generated texts will not force the writer to retype the entire draft (18). And using computers in conjunction with peer editing is advantageous whether students are typing their comments directly onto the text or writing their comments on printed hard copies: the neatness of the hard copies eliminates the difficulty of commenting on hard-to-read papers (18). Still another possibility is the overhead transparency. The transparency invites whole-class participation in peer review and is again facilitated by the neatness of the typed copy.

Peckham offers further suggestions for peer editing. One suggestion—for those whose computers make it possible—is the use of color, such as blue for strikeouts and red for additions (336). Color-coding offers the additional benefit of distinguishing the peer reviewers' comments from the original text. Having students put their initials before or after comments or having them comment in all capital letters are two other possibilities.

Most of the discussion to this point paints computer-assisted peer review in its best light. But while the computer does enhance the peer review process in some ways, it also creates its own set of complications. To begin with, in order for students to trade disks and open up each other's texts, the instructor must arrange the classroom or writing lab so that all students are using compatible disks, compatible computers, and compatible word-processing programs. Once this obstacle is overcome, the next chore the instructor faces is the task of file management. In the case of peer editing, two versions of a student's text must exist simultaneously: the original text and the student-edited text. The creation of a second file for editing purposes usually entails the renaming of that second file, either with an addition to the original title or recast in all caps. Here are two examples:

1. original file: My Essay   file for editing: My Essay, edit
2. original file: My Essay   file for editing: MY ESSAY

Ensuring that systems are compatible and that a viable file-saving system is in place may seem a difficult enough task. Yet further questions present themselves: Will I give credit for the quality and/or quantity of peer review a student does? If so, how? How much of the writing process do I want to oversee? Do I want to see earlier drafts? All drafts? Some drafts? Do I want to see the draft(s) that contains the peer review comments? How do students decide when to print? And how do I dole out credit for all this? True, we could read about how others have solved these and other organizational issues. But that would take the fun out of it. Teaching writing is the easy part; it is in the oft-overlooked arena of devising classroom systems and infrastructure that, through our innate re-sourcefulness and inspiration, we as teachers can really shine.

We have now examined constructivism, the driving theory behind computer-assisted writing instruction. We've discussed constructivism as theory and as an extension of politics. We've delved into constructivism as it manifests itself in the computer-based writing classroom—components such as student-centered instruction, collaborative learning, small groups, and peer response. We've made an initial study of how peer response might be implemented in the classroom and the difficulties created by the computers themselves. Before we turn to the question of whether computers improve student writing—the pivotal issue within the discipline—we have two last constructivist-related issues to explore: (1) how campus-based politics might affect a teacher's attempt to teach writing based on the constructivist model and (2) the possible speciousness of constructivism as an educational model.

Campus Politics

In truth, constructivist classrooms can flourish only if allowed to do so by the powers that be—the policymakers at the state and federal levels and the administration at district and campus levels. For these policymakers, the current operative word is *standards.* These standards, depending on what you read and whom you talk to, are alternately described as "progressive" and as "back-to-basics." Since the standards are assembled by committees that contain partisans from both camps, we may safely assume that whatever the final form these standards do take they will contain both progressive and back-to-basics elements. It's the back-to-basics elements that bode potential ill for practitioners of constructivism. Back-to-basics curricula and standardized tests and/or exit exams would severely limit the freedom of any teacher to practice constructivist learning in the classroom. The pressure would most likely come from administrators who want to look good by publicly touting the school's high scores on the latest standardized test. Teachers who have chosen to focus less on furnishing students with factual information and more on students constructing their own learning—on learning how to learn—will be seen as hindering the achievement of higher scores on standardized tests. Some speak of using standardized test scores to evaluate teachers, but whether this will become a reality remains to be seen.

In their 1994 article "English under Pressure: Back to Basics?" Sally Tweddle and Phil Moore address this very issue. They propose that forward-thinking teachers rally together to "find a formula for representing to others what it is that we are doing" (284). The key is to steal back the word *basic* from the back-to-basics camp and redefine it. "Basic" skills such as reading and writing are "possible only in the context of knowledge about and understanding of those modes of meaning making and the processes they involve" (284). Tweddle and Moore suggest that elements of constructivism and technology be reconsidered as basics. Among these elements are "developing in students the ability to understand and respond critically to what is written" (285); "enabling them to understand and to enter into the reader-writer relationship" (285); and "enabling them to understand processes of writing that others engage in and to write themselves" (285). In addition to viewing these deeper understandings of literacy as basic, Tweddle and Moore also insist that "computers and computer-related writing and composing tools" and "literacy skills . . . that relate to electronic media" (285) be redefined as components of getting back to basics.

Against Constructivism

Theory informs practice, and the practice of computer-assisted writing instruction is informed by the theory of constructivism. This is made clear by the preponderance of journal articles within the discipline that, instead of undertaking to delineate this alliance, *assume* this alliance as an axiom and base further reflection on it. But is computer-assisted writing instruction best served by constructivism? Opinion to the contrary is difficult to find, but it does exist. Peckham concedes that there is no evidence to support the efficacy of peer response (328) and that a potential drawback of peer response is the possibility that students might not possess the requisite knowledge to ably assist their peers (328). Williams warns that "collaboration may be discontinued if failure, challenge to authority, and/ or the time required to 'master' the technology becomes overwhelming" (43). Marilyn Jody and Marianne Saccardi warn against losing "the heart of the humanities, literature itself" (vii), a concern echoed by Todd Oppenheimer, who would have us return to a "broad liberal-arts curricula . . . instead of focusing on today's idea about what tomorrow's jobs will be" (55). Perhaps the most vocal and notable apologist of the traditional, anticonstructivist camp is E. D. Hirsch, of cultural literacy fame.

In his book *The Schools We Need and Why We Don't Have Them*, Hirsch challenges the tenets of progressive education. Hirsch counters those who would present progressive education as a new solution to old problems by arguing that progressivist theories have been with us since as early as 1918. Progressivism, therefore, is not a recent theoretical innovation but an entrenched movement that has been given nearly a century to produce results, which it has failed to do (48). Hirsch characterizes progressivism as an "anti-knowledge" (54) doctrine grounded in romanticism and characterized by such components as critical thinking, self-esteem, and attention to the individual—three educational approaches that, paradoxically, bring results in direct opposition to their intended results (66). Hirsch also challenges progressive educational theory in the very arena in which it might have felt most secure—research. Hirsch claims that "the findings of research emphatically do not accord with the 'reforms' currently being recommended by the educational community. In fact, many reformers have neglected mainstream research in favor of nonconsensus theories . . . that happen to support progressivist goals and methods" (131). Hirsch points out that we should place greater faith in the findings of "refereed journals in mainstream disciplines" (265) and "studies of definitely observable effects exhibited by large populations of subjects over considerable periods of time" (266). Citing such large-scale studies from mainstream refereed journals, Hirsch concludes that the qualities of truly effective teachers stand in direct contradiction to the qualities espoused by the advocates of constructivism, including a "sustained focus on content" and "whole class instruction" (161). Instead of leaving students to fend for themselves ("student-centered learning"), it is the teacher's duty to impart "intellectual capital" (17) and "shared knowledge" (22). Hirsch asserts that in reality it is through imparting intellectual capital and shared knowledge that we achieve the democratic ideal of raising the poor and disenfranchised to a more desirable social position (43).

Avoiding the Two Extremes

Theorists have wedded computer-assisted writing instruction with progressive, constructivist notions of teaching writing. These theorists are opposed to using computers as a mere prosthesis in maintaining the status quo in our writing classrooms. Instead, they see the computer as an instrument of complete transformation—metamorphosing the acts of writing and writing instruction, thoroughly altering the teacher-student relationship, and compelling us to reconsider the intrinsic foundations that have long defined the teaching of composition. But, we must ask, is the fusing of computer-assisted writing instruction with constructivism an inevitable match? Perhaps not. Perhaps the newness of computers should lead us not into newness of theory but into a return to the traditional:

With the perplexing task before us of integrating computer technology with print and oral traditions, now is hardly the time for the teacher to step aside and become what the wide-eyed technophiles call "the guide on the side." We have a responsibility to preserve from the old what is dear to us as well as to discover in the new what is truly beneficial. (Monke, "Web and the Plow" 34)

Ultimately, our wisest course is to trust to the middle ground. One need not teach writing in a fashion blindly partisan to one camp or the other. Constructivist teaching and a "directive approach" (Rohan 21) are two complementary instructional styles. Optimally, the teacher of composition would integrate the two styles and reap the benefits of each. Through constructivist pedagogy, the student is empowered through the act of personal meaning making. But when we wish to "introduce skills or concepts, build awareness, or reinforce some set of actions that can be replayed habitually," or when we want to "cover the necessary content in a given amount of time" (Sandholtz, Ringstaff, and Dwyer 14)—then direct instruction becomes the more appropriate pedagogy.

The question arises: which areas of composition instruction are best suited for direct instruction? In a later section of this book, we study this question in greater detail. But before deciding which components of composition instruction are best suited for direct instruction with computers, it behooves us to first examine two more primary questions:

1. What are the advantages of using computers to teach writing?
2. Where do we draw the line between what computers *can* do and what they *cannot* do?

2 Using Computers to Teach Writing: Advantages and Disadvantages

When considering whether to introduce computers into the writing classroom, one question stands above the rest: do computers improve the writing of students? The answer, surprisingly, is that we don't know. Wolfe et al. report that "researchers do not agree about the effects of using word processors on the quality of student writing" (270). Owston, Murphy, and Wideman inform us that "the results to date have been equivocal" (251). Joram et al. tell us that, in regard to the accepted belief that computers facilitate revision, "there is little research that directly tests this claim" (168). Collier and Werier find that "research on the qualitative changes effected in writing by word-processing systems have been either contradictory or inconclusive . . . for all population samples—experienced professional and academic writers, as well as several categories of inexperienced writers" (47).

Despite the questionable ability of the computer to elicit improvement at the general level of "writing improvement," the computer does improve student writing at certain more specific levels. If we were to break the act of writing into its more specific constituent parts, we could then reformulate our original question: which particular components of the writing process are improved by using computers? Once we have analyzed the effect of computers on the various constituent parts of the overall act of writing, we will be in a better position to decide whether the pros of computer-assisted writing instruction outweigh the cons.

What Computers Can and Cannot Do

As we wade through one professional journal after another, the advantages of computer-assisted writing instruction begin to pile up, as do the disadvantages. Only through weighing and comparing these pros and cons can we ultimately determine the value of computers in the writing classroom; but before we enter any such discussion, let's take an at-a-glance look at the pros and cons in list form:

The Pros (as Compared to Students Writing with Pen and Paper)

Students:

- write better (Pennington 59)
- produce longer texts (Wolfe et al. 270; Kantrov 63; Pennington 59; Hawisher 11)
- produce neater texts; take pride in the neatness of texts (Wolfe et al. 270; Kantrov 70)
- produce more error-free texts (Wolfe et al. 270; Kantrov 63; Hawisher 10)
- are more empowered, see themselves as individuals who are "in print" (Gruber 29; Kalmbach 59)
- take more initiative; spend more time on assignments and more time on task; are more involved with assignments (Sandholtz, Ringstaff, and Dwyer 90, 94; Sabik 49)
- are more willing to experiment and take risks (Sandholtz, Ringstaff, and Dwyer 96; Kantrov 65–66)
- show more enthusiasm, more positive attitudes (Kantrov 63; Pennington 60; Hawisher 13; Sandholtz, Ringstaff, and Dwyer 90–91; Crafton 318)
- are more distanced from text; more likely to tap into authorial self as distinct from the actual self (Dowling 230–31)
- display more engagement with text (Collier and Werier 51)
- are more aware of recursiveness and the writing process (Takayoshi 247; Collier and Werier 51)
- gain a clearer, more well-defined sense of audience (Owston, Murphy, and Wideman 250; Wolfe et al. 270; Sandholtz, Ringstaff, and Dwyer 13; Takayoshi 247)
- are more able and willing to revise (Owston, Murphy, and Wideman 249; Kantrov 64; Pennington 60; Monroe 48–49; Sabik 49; Klonoski 74; Collier and Werier 47)
- are more able and willing to read one another's writing or engage in peer review (Owston, Murphy, and Wideman 250; Dowling 228; Wolfe et al. 270), to collaborate (Hawisher 16; Takayoshi 247), to interact socially (Wolfe et al. 270; Rohan 21; Takayoshi 247), and to forge a unified class identity (Sands 37)
- are better prepared for the business/industry world or the "real" world (Ruenzel 26; Cuban, Foreword xi)

Other advantages:

- easier for the teacher to intervene/coach (due to the neat, orderly presentation of text on a monitor) (Rohan 20–21)

- advantageous for basic writers: more initiative (Sandholtz, Ringstaff, and Dwyer 95); able to delete sources of embarrassment (Kantrov 65); improved writing (Hawisher 14)

The Cons (as Compared to Students Writing with Pen and Paper)

- increased difficulty for basic writers (Crafton 318, 323–25)
- difficulty in providing direct instruction due to difficulty drawing students' attention away from computers (Ruenzel 28); the computer can be a distraction (Sandholtz, Ringstaff, and Dwyer 59)
- inequitable access to computers: more access for the rich, less for the poor; also, low-achieving students are more likely to use computers for drill-and-skill, less likely to use computers for writing or holistic problem solving (Cuban, Foreword xi)
- more clutter in the classroom (Sandholtz, Ringstaff, and Dwyer 60)
- more downtime (Sandholtz, Ringstaff, and Dwyer 60)
- monotony; difficulty sustaining students' interest (Sandholtz, Ringstaff, and Dwyer 97, 102)
- potential dependencies created through prolonged use of word processor (Collier and Werier 48)
- less writing for pleasure, such as letter writing (Dowling 234)
- a technocentric attitude: students deduce that the equipment is more important than the teacher (Crafton 321)
- an increased vulnerability to business interests and the "commercial/technological alliance" that hopes to enlist future workers and consumers (Monke, "Web and the Plow" 34)
- less prewriting (Hawisher 16); less outlining (Kantrov 67)
- a distorted sense of audience: the computer becomes the audience; an impersonal, nonhuman audience replaces a human audience (Heilker 65–68; Dowling 231–32; Crafton 324)

Revision-centered problems:

- Students confuse revision with error correction (Crafton 322; Joram et al. 169).
- Tinkering with surface-level error correction while in the process of drafting results in poorer writing (Joram et al. 169–70; Heilker 61, 63; Klonoski 73–74; Dowling 233; Crafton 318, 319, 325; Kantrov 66; Sharples 222).
- Students actually do less revision because they don't have to recopy (Kantrov 64).

- Revision is made more difficult due to small screen size (Dowling 228).
- Text closure, due to ease of editing, is more difficult to reach (Dowling 232).

Students write more poorly due to:

- small screen size and seeing only a small part of the text (Kantrov 68; Owston, Murphy, and Wideman 250; Takayoshi 253)
- more focus on "product" features of word processing (such as font) as opposed to the "process" of quality text (Crafton 319; Kantrov 70; Sandholtz, Ringstaff, and Dwyer 98; Dowling 230)
- computers causing "memory overload" (Joram et al. 190)

This list summary is meant to provide an overview of the advantages and disadvantages of writing with computers. But within this general framework, certain issues stand out as more prominent than the rest and worth closer study. These are the issues of revision, audience, the business world, writing with pen and paper, social interaction, and attitude/enthusiasm. We now look at each of these issues in turn.

Revision

At one time, proponents of computer-assisted writing instruction claimed ease of revision as an obvious and indisputable advantage of using computers to teach writing. Today, certain revision-based drawbacks to using word processors have been identified. One drawback is that word processing, because it allows text to be so easily manipulated, lends itself more readily to surface-level or local-level revision than to deep revision. Therefore, student writers are far more likely to engage in surface-level revision. Ultimately, they begin to equate error correction with revision.

This increased concentration on surface-level revision[1] carries with it the concomitant problem of decreased concentration not only on deep revision, but also on the initial stage of text generation itself. Too much involvement with "evaluation early in the creative process may interfere with the fluidity that is necessary for generating ideas" (Joram et al. 169). Carolyn Dowling has noticed a disturbing trend among students and professional writers alike, finding that writers composing on word processors are frequently producing texts that—perhaps due to excessive cut-and-paste—appear to be "an aggregation of modules of text" that lack "conceptual flow and stylistic coherence" (233).

Features such as cut-and-paste, delete, insert, spellcheck, and grammar check may be redefining the concept of revision for the worse.

Meanwhile, another set of word-processing features—those that modify and amend the appearance of text on the page—might be whispering their own deceitful innuendo in the minds of student writers. Writing students who manipulate such functions as font size, font style, boldface, margin justification, bullets, and text centering are being given the "illusory impression of productivity" (Dowling 230) and being taught the lessons of "artwork and layout over content" and "glitz over guts" (Sandholtz, Ringstaff, and Dwyer 98). James Kalmbach reminds us that "students have always found ways to fixate on appearance rather than content" (58). These students are not entirely to blame, for they believe themselves to be imitating "what they perceive to be the values of literate society" (58). For the past few decades, this obsession with neatness as a virtue has been fueled by the existence of the comparatively low-tech Liquid Paper. Computers have taken this cult of neatness as symbolized by Liquid Paper and raised the stakes many times over. The result could be a generation of student writers who, due to the slickness of their word processor–generated writing, produce writing that lacks quality and depth because of a premature sense of smugness with their texts.

We have seen that a student writer's infatuation with "displacement activities" (Sharples 222)—spellcheck, word counting, grammar check, etc.—can have three negative results for writers:

1. allowing local-area revision to replace deep revision
2. diminishing the creativity and logical continuity that should be the chief characteristic of the prewriting or drafting stage of writing
3. lending a false sense of security in which the neatness or slickness of computer-generated text gives the impression of quality writing

To these three, we might add a fourth negative result: the disturbance of rhythm. Rhythm in the writing process is the pattern of alternating periods of active writing with periods of reflection. In "Computer Support for the Rhythms of Writing," Mike Sharples points out that though different writers employ different rhythms, all writers must bolster their writing with periods of reflection. But with the advent of word processing, the reflective stages of a writer's rhythm are now replaced by the writer's puttering with the various text-manipulating features that the word processor offers. The result is that "the rhythms of writing are becoming ever more complex and syncopated" (222). Sharples also expresses concern that future word processors "will offer yet more movements away from the text" (222) with innovations such as the dynamic outlining option of Microsoft Word.

But enough of blaming the technology. Much of the blame for the revision problems that the advent of computers has now amplified rests with us—teachers of composition at all levels. In his "Revision Worship and the Computer as Audience," Paul Heilker traces the evolution of revision as a good idea gone bad. We began by focusing on writing as a process, followed by a focus on revision, followed by the collaborative workshop, "the teaching method by which we could promote and, indeed, attempt to insure such revisions" (61). Process, revision, and the collaborative workshop—three terms that most teachers of writing invest with positive connotations. The problem, Heilker points out, is that what should be natural and organic has become synthetic and institutionalized. Through the medium of the collaborative workshop, we *schedule* revision, which in turn "rips revision out of a holistic, continually recursive notion of writing process and firmly plants it in a linear one" (62). Computers have only exacerbated the situation. Because computers have eased the revision process—a task once associated with drudgery—we are now far more likely to set aside certain class periods for scheduled revisions. And to cap it all off, students who revise receive higher grades than those who don't, thus promoting the objectionable student practice of revising for grades. All of this amounts to a series of messages to students that would be better off unsent: "that revision is always a good, productive thing; that revision is a worthwhile end or goal in and of itself; that every text needs to be or should be revised; that revision comes after writing as a separate, often last stage in a linear process" (63).

Audience

The issue of audience—much like the issue of revision—elicits mixed responses. There are those who say that using computers to teach writing augments and more sharply defines a student's sense of audience. A recent study conducted by Edward Wolfe et al. concludes that "students who chose to take their writing assessment on a word processor were more likely to look at the writing of other students than students who took the writing assessment with pen and paper" (270). Sandholtz, Ringstaff, and Dwyer believe that the computer is superior to pen and paper in permitting the student to overcome "privately held constructions" (13). A student's writing "needs to be reviewed by peers, explained to parents, presented to expert panels, considered for entry into personal portfolios, and reviewed and assessed against rigorous standards" (13). The computer—with its polished product, its publishing capacities, and its adaptability to peer review—is an ideal tool for turning "privately held constructions" into public discourse.

Heilker and Dowling, on the other hand, in what might seem like recourse to science fiction, view the computer as competing with the student writer's endeavor to formulate an audience—competing to such a degree that "the writer-computer relationship is displacing and replacing the writer-audience relationship in the rhetorical situation" (Heilker 65). Dowling describes writers who "are in the curious position of constituting themselves as manifested on the computer screen and, in this sense, may be seen as constituting the computer to a significant degree in their own image" (232). One danger of the computer-as-audience is an acquired sense of "talking" to the computer, which in turn results in "an excessively informal prose style."

Heilker notes two definitions of audience: (1) "audience-addressed," the real-life human beings who will read the text, and (2) "audience-invoked," the audience that the writer imagines himself or herself to be writing to (66). It is the place of the invoked audience that the computer may be usurping. Heilker hypothesizes that the pseudohuman thinking qualities of computers allow us to readily invest them with human qualities: "But because we can and do somehow easily identify with our computers as intelligent beings (responders, commentators, questioners, teachers, collaborators, and allies)—as our audiences—we need not and do not engage other people to achieve that identification, to overcome that separateness" (67). The concern, of course, is that if computers *are* invading territory once reserved for human beings, we run the risk of losing the human dimension of writing, even of losing some of our own humanity.

Ties to Business: Ethical Questions

It would be highly naive for anyone to believe that all computers that materialize on campuses across our country and all monies earmarked for technology are the gifts of beneficent donors interested only in the advancement of education. The truth is that more often than not if a business or especially a computer company invests money in our schools, it makes that investment in the expectation of some future return.

Teacher opinion about the link between computers and business falls mainly into one of two categories. Those of us who take a more pragmatic view or who appreciate the value of vocational education are more likely to support the computer–business connection. Others of us—due either to our idealism or to our skepticism—see any links between schools and business as evils against which unwitting students should be defended.

David Ruenzel is of this first category. In his "Is This the Future of Education in America?" he depicts New Technology High in Napa Valley as a high school overtly "modeled after a high-tech business start-up" (25). At New Technology High, students are groomed for the business world with the skills of the business world: "basic technology skills, a willingness to work in teams, and the ability to apply knowledge to real-world projects" (26). From this perspective, those of us who use computers to teach writing might easily congratulate ourselves with the thought that while we are teaching writing, we are simultaneously preparing our students for the business world. On the other hand, it might be just as easy to fret about whether we might be selling out to business interests. A campus is—or is supposed to be—a neutral ground, free and untainted by the commercial interests of business, industry, and advertising. But because so many schools are unable to afford the number of computers they want or need, various business interests find that the computer is a most efficient worm with which to bait the hook. Once business interests have insinuated themselves into the fabric of our schools, curricula itself become vulnerable; and "if business gains too much influence over the curriculum, the schools can become a kind of corporate training center—largely at taxpayer expense" (Oppenheimer 55). The warning is clear: once we have welcomed computers into our writing classrooms, we assume an ancillary responsibility "to protect the interests of the children in our care against the commercial/technological alliance that too often cares more about education as a market than as a servant of children's needs" (Monke, "Web and the Plow" 34).

Pro–Word Processor

In this section, we compare writing with a word processor to writing with pen and paper, underscoring the advantages of the word processor. At first glance, pitting the low-tech pen against the high-tech word processor might seem like pitting David against Goliath—or more accurately, pitting John Henry against the steam shovel. But perhaps surprisingly, many are the voices rooting for David and John Henry, and we examine their perspective in the section following this one.

Of course, the advantages of the word processor over pen and paper are many and obvious, especially to those of us who have left behind "the barriers extant in an older technology" (Monroe 1) and who do all our composing on computers.[2] Ease of revision is perhaps the most prominent advantage. True, the previous section on revision sets forth numerous arguments questioning the effectiveness of revising with computers, but those arguments are directed against the computer itself, not against the computer as compared to pen and paper. Owston, Murphy, and Wideman report that "the work of rewriting by hand may be a serious impediment to revising" (249). The advantage of the computer is not just that it allows for "far easier text modification," but that it removes "the drudgery of recopying a composition" (250).

Ease of revision is one difference between computers and pen and paper. Another is text neatness. With the computer, the playing field has been leveled: those with poor handwriting are now judged on the same basis as those with neat handwriting. The result is that the producers of any text will be evaluated on content only, which is as it should be. Naturally, students are aware of the appearance factor; Wolfe et al. report that, due to the neater appearance of the text, "students favor writing with a word processor when their writing will be read for informative or evaluative purposes, such as a writing assessment" (280).

The use of computers for writing assessments may be an overlooked issue. If we run a computer-based composition classroom, fairness and consistency would dictate that students be given the option of word processing for assessment. This same principle should also be applied to standardized testing, for which handwritten tests are the norm. In "Writing a Wrong," Jack McGarvey pleads for the conversion of handwritten standardized tests into word-processing-optional standardized tests. McGarvey is "utterly convinced that handwritten tests do not accurately measure the quality of kids' writing" (52). He tells of a group of students who, "after experiencing the ease and speed of touch typing . . . were frustrated that they now had to write with something so crude as a pen" (52). For those of us who would like to see students using word processors in all writing situations, a reasonable course to follow would be to allow word processing whenever it is within our power to do so and, in the case of standardized tests, to agitate for change.

Of course, we must also avoid the extreme of enforced word processing in writing for assessment or in standardized writing tests. Some students may prefer pen and paper. In a test conducted by Richard Collier and Clifford Werier, students writing in both the pen-and-paper and the computer modes were given equal scores on various sets of essays (56).

Pro–Pen and Paper

In the previous section, we enumerated the advantages of the computer over the pen. We now examine those grounds on which pen and paper might be considered superior to the computer.

Although writing with a computer has many advantages, with our entry into the high-tech environment of composing with computers something is lost as well. What we have gained is a writing form described as "less personal" (Kantrov 71). What we have lost is a writing form described as more "physical" and that provides more "closeness" (Chandler 194); that provides "the pleasure of bodily involvement" (Berry 192); that yields an "intelligence in the hands" and a "kinesthetic way of knowing" (Chandler 195); that allows more "intimate contact" with the text; and that allows us to "feel the rhythms, the syntax, the word choices in ways that reading will not allow" (Crafton 325).

In "Who Needs Suspended Inscription?" Chandler explores more thoroughly the tangible, physical nature of handwritten text, positing that it is the romantic nature in us that sees "the process of generating text . . . as least as important as . . . the eventual product" (194). As we generate text, we engage in the process of discovery. Through the medium of handwritten text, our discovery process has always had a tactile, physical component. We have, perhaps in some metaphysical way, used the body as a medium for thinking. Without the reassuring material nature of the pen and paper, it would follow that our initial process of converting thought into writing by means of computer is inferior to what it was before.

Another conjectural point of comparison arises from the issue of speed. Chandler suggests that the speed with which word-processed thoughts reach paper might impinge on the depth of those thoughts. With the word processor, the danger exists of writing *too* quickly, of writing without allowing sufficient time for reflection, for "dwelling on," or "mulling over," the text.

Finally, Chandler suggests that the small size of the computer screen disrupts a text's unity. Those writers who prefer to "spread out their sheets of writing in front of them on a desk, floor or wall seem . . . to get a better sense of the shape of their text and of their ideas as manipulable, physical objects" (197–98). Such writers are unable to tackle the job of major revision until they have first printed a hard copy of their texts.

A Place for Both

Several studies approach the word processor versus pen and paper question not to demonstrate that one mode of writing is superior to the other but to compare the strengths and weaknesses of the two modes. Recognizing that each of the two modes of writing is better suited to certain types of writing has led some teachers "to encourage students to develop their own combinations of pencil and paper and computer-writing strategies" (Rodrigues and Rodrigues 16). Tenth-grade students of varying levels of writing ability were the subjects of a test conducted by Edward Wolfe et al. The students were asked which mode of writing they would choose for informative writing, which for narrative writing, and which for personal writing. The results: 80 percent of the students would use the word processor for informative writing; 83 percent would use pen and paper for personal writing. Narrative writing fell equidistant between the two at 50 percent.

In a more sustained comparison between the two modes of writing, Daniel Chandler makes these observations:

- The word processor is faster, though revision might slow down the final product.
- Pen and paper is more "direct and immediate"; word processing is more "indirect and delayed."
- Pen and paper provide "immediate availability of whole text on paper"; word processing provides "selective access to text" (due to the small screen) and "delayed access to text on paper."
- Text is easier to edit and to reorganize with word processing.
- When revision is necessary, text produced with a word processor does not require rewriting.
- Revision in pen "preserves" the evolution of the text; word processing "obscures" the evolution (192).

Based on these comparisons and on a survey of professional writers, Daniel Chandler derives a continuum of writing choices ranging from personal to public. He postulates that most writers have "a sense of a pen or pencil as appropriate for more personal writing and of a typewriter or a word processor as appropriate for more public writing" (193). Chandler also notes that in many cases the two modes of writing can be mutually beneficial. When the two modes are used together to produce a single text, writers will most often use pen and paper for the "tentative initial phases" of producing texts and use word processing for "later stages in the development of ideas," stages that are "associated with greater formality" (193).

Social Interaction

According to the constructivist credo, a proper composition classroom is marked by increased social interaction among the students. It might seem that the very nature of the computer itself would tend to make each student's experience in the classroom a more solitary one, but several studies report that this is not so. Perhaps due to the ease with which one student can read the writing of another, computers tend to promote collaboration among students. Gail Hawisher notes "a spirit of cooperation rather than of competitiveness prevail[ing] in a classroom with computers" (16). Pamela Takayoshi calls computer-assisted composition "more public" and, again, more "collaborative and social" (247). Peter Sands describes how "a class can develop a new sense of itself as a group striving together" (37). Liz Rohan takes the idea of social interaction and extends the boundaries to include the teacher, who, in the environment of the computer-assisted composition classroom, finds himself or herself spending more time directly coaching students. All four of these writers agree that although the computer itself promotes sharing and collaboration among students, it is still the teacher's responsibility to employ pedagogy that takes full advantage of the computer's potential for producing collaboration.

Attitude/Enthusiasm

Most students display a positive attitude toward word processing, which in turn is converted into a better opinion of writing itself (Hawisher 13). Sandholtz, Ringstaff, and Dwyer, reporting on the Apple Classrooms of Tomorrow (ACOT) project, laud the technology-intensive classrooms, the laptops for all students provided by ACOT, and the many advantages brought about by writing with computers—especially the advantage of improved attitudes among students. The authors inform us that "students learned more quickly" and that "their interest reinforced [the] teacher's efforts" (90). Teachers reported a myriad of welcome changes in student behavior, among them an unflagging willingness to work up until the last day of school, an unwillingness to return the computers at collection time, and an increased enrollment in computer-based classes.

My own experience corroborates Sandholtz, Ringstaff, and Dwyer's observations. After taking three classes of ninth graders into a Macintosh computer lab (Maclab) over a period of two or three months, I asked the students to write on the topic "Writing with Computers." No other instructions were given. Out of eighty-eight responses, only three were unfavorable, each of the three for the same reason—poor typing skills and/or confusion with the word-processing program. The other eighty-five students favored doing their writing on computers. The reasons for preferring computers, in descending frequency of response, were these:

- Spellcheck and/or grammar check. Students expressed little confidence in their own abilities to produce text that wasn't teeming with errors.

- Neatness or the professional look. Many students indicated that they appreciated the way the computer helped them overcome the obstacle of their poor handwriting.

- Fun. Writing on computers is more enjoyable than writing by hand.

- The vocational connection. Many students indicated that they were glad to be using computers because in "real life" they would be using computers. Our trips to the Maclab were seen as practice for functioning more competently in "the world of tomorrow."

- The virtual text. Some students appreciated the cut, paste, delete, and insert functions of the computer. Students can accomplish all these functions without crossing out or erasing, leaving them with "neat" text. Also, they need not carry around a sheet of paper or have to remember where that paper is; instead, the next time they need to access that text, it is waiting in the computer.

Summary

This book argues that composition instructors *should* favor using computers to teach writing, while at the same time avoiding the overly idealistic attitude that computers are the panacea for all pedagogical difficulties. As such, this chapter looks honestly at the place of computers in writing instruction. After weighing both the advantages and disadvantages of computer-assisted writing instruction—first a more superficial glance presented in list form and then a more in-depth discussion of certain prominent issues, we discovered that, even when the advantage of the computer over pen and paper is indisputable—during revision, for example—some questions regarding the efficacy of computer use yet remain. In a direct comparison of computer-assisted writing with pen and paper, we see that pen and paper still has its place in the writing classroom—for specific tasks, under certain conditions. We would do well to maintain in our classrooms the flexibility for students to choose the writing mode they feel most comfortable with.

The argument most damning to computer-assisted writing instruction is that despite the enthusiasm with which we continue to stock our classrooms with computers, research shows that students who write on computers show little or no improvement in the quality of their writing.

On the other hand, one cannot discount the enthusiasm with which students engage in computer-assisted writing as opposed to writing with pen and paper.

Do the advantages outweigh the disadvantages? Do we allow the importance of greater student enthusiasm to outweigh the research regarding lack of writing improvement? An answer to this question lies in the theory and pedagogy of Daniel Fader's *The New Hooked on Books*. Fader argues that pleasure alone should dictate what K–12 students read. Most students, however, rather than being allowed to read books that interest them, are force-fed a diet of canon-only texts. True, some students thrive on a diet of the classics, but many or most only learn to dislike reading. Teaching the canon is a case of good intentions, bad results. Fader suggests that students be allowed to read for pleasure. Schools should be flooded with paperbacks and, ideally, we would see kids all over campus, readers and ex-non-readers alike, with books stuffed into their back pockets. These students, through reading books that many literature purists would consider to be of dubious merit, would learn to enjoy reading. Eventually, this love of reading would carry over into their later years. In contrast to the canon-fed students who stop reading forever upon high school graduation, the students who read for pleasure will develop a habit of lifelong reading. Paradoxically, these same students who read for pleasure stand a good chance of becoming the readers of classics and other quality fiction and nonfiction; as long as they continue to read, the possibility exists that they may be weaned off milk and onto meat.

If the do-it-for-enjoyment principle can be applied to reading, it seems logical that it could be applied to writing as well. If our students leave our classrooms with a distaste for writing, the fact that they may have learned something about writing will, in the long run, matter little. Conversely, if students learn to enjoy writing, it matters little whether computers *improve* student writing or not. What matters is that students *will* write; and over a lifetime of pursuing a pleasurable habit, they will improve as writers. Enthusiasm and attitude, then, constitute the overarching justification for using computers to teach writing. And once the decision to use computers has been settled, the next subject we turn our attention to is the person responsible for seeing that the computers be put to their best use—the teacher. The next chapter examines the teacher's role in computer-assisted writing instruction in three sections that move from the general to the concrete. First we examine the position of the teacher him- or herself in connection with the decision to "go high tech"; then we move from the teacher to the general principles of teaching with computers; and finally we move into the most practical domain of all—specific lesson plans.

3 Teachers

*Until they [teachers] decide how, where and under what conditions computers
are allocated, students' use of classroom technologies will be occasional and
marginal. Only teachers can integrate the use of computers with the subject
matter and skills that they are expected to teach and upon which students are
tested. Unfortunately, it is policy-makers and administrators, save for a token
teacher here and there, who make the key decisions about using computers in
schools. (Cuban, "Unless")*

The gist of these words from Larry Cuban is that teachers are the foundation on which the use of computers in education is built. Teachers need to understand the importance of their position and take a proactive, rather than a reactive, stance toward using computers in the classroom. But, according to Cuban, this is not happening, for four reasons:

1. Teachers are not included in the decision making; in fact, they are the last link in the decision-making chain that begins with governors and legislators, is then passed on to school boards and superintendents, is then passed on to principals, and is finally dropped in the lap of teachers.

2. "Teachers have yet to be convinced that all students learn more, better and faster with computers."

3. Software programs are inconsistent and rarely "match existing curriculum or annual tests."

4. "Equipment . . . often breaks down and there is seldom help to get the machines up and running again promptly" (Cuban, "Unless").

If teachers are going to take control of the reins and decide for themselves how and to what extent technology will figure in the education formula for the years ahead, they must first develop a procomputer attitude. We might suspect that the ranks of teachers include more Luddite and antitechnology sentiment than that found on average in the general public. To better discover whether an antitechnology attitude is common among teachers, I sent a survey to every English teacher in the school district in which I teach. Forty-eight teachers responded, just less than 50 percent of the teachers solicited. The survey consists of ten questions rated on a scale of 1 to 6, 1 meaning *strongly disagree,* 6 meaning *strongly agree.* Here are the results of that survey. The number of 1 responses is listed to the left; the number of 6 responses is listed to the right; an X indicates that no one selected that number as a response:

1. I believe that it's important to equip English teachers with computers/word processors and/or to make computer labs more available for English teachers to use.

   | 1 | X | 2 | 2 | 8 | 34 |

2. I see computers as more of a glamorous toy than an integral part of English instruction, and I don't foresee making instructional use of computers.

   | 23 | 7 | 7 | 2 | 6 | 1 |

3. I would like to make more use of computers/word processors, but I'm limited by not having any/enough computers or by lack of availability.

   | 2 | 2 | 4 | 3 | 12 | 25 |

4. I would like to make more use of computers/word processors, but I'm limited by lack of computer experience and/or proper training.

   | 10 | 9 | 7 | 15 | 5 | 1 |

5. I have taken my classes to write on computers/word processors in a lab situation, and I feel the experience was time well spent.

   | 3 | 1 | 3 | 8 | 6 | 18 |

   (not applicable = 8)

6. I am in favor of students doing their writing assignments on computers/word processors rather than with pen and paper.

   | X | 1 | 5 | 10 | 7 | 23 |

7. I believe that English teachers in our district should incorporate into the classroom lessons that involve students using word processing.

   | X | 3 | 1 | 5 | 9 | 29 |

8. I believe that English teachers in our district should incorporate into the classroom lessons that involve students using the Internet.

   | 4 | 3 | 5 | 10 | 8 | 18 |

9. I believe that English teachers in our district should incorporate into the classroom lessons that involve students communicating via e-mail.

   | 5 | 6 | 4 | 10 | 4 | 15 |

10. I believe that English teachers in our district should incorporate into the classroom lessons that involve students producing multimedia creations; e.g., desktop publishing, homepages, PowerPoint demonstrations, etc.

    | 1 | 1 | 1 | 7 | 11 | 23 |

From the results of this survey, we can draw the following conclusions about teachers in this district; assuming that these forty-eight respondents are a fair representation of teachers everywhere, we might also extend these conclusions to be true of teachers in general:

1. Teachers want to use computers.
2. Teachers are more limited by lack of access than by lack of training.
3. Teachers favor having students write with word processors.
4. Teachers favor making full use of the computer's various functions: the Internet, e-mail, desktop publishing, homepages, PowerPoint demonstrations, etc.

Beginnings

Undoubtedly, teachers who plan on making computers an integral part of their pedagogy must first have their own computers. Teachers whose only computers are those in their classrooms do not have the time or the resources to learn the various computer applications, nor the time to plan teaching lessons that employ computers. For teachers to really become comfortable with transforming their traditional classrooms into computer-based classrooms, they must own their own computers. Daily computer use will unlock possibilities for using the computer in the classroom, for teachers will not value the learning students might do with computers until they use one in their professional lives.

Granted, teachers should own computers. One way for a teacher to own a computer is, of course, to buy one. The problem with this solution is that teachers make teachers' salaries. Another solution to the problem of getting computers into the hands of teachers is for the schools to provide them. The South Huntington School District in New York sees this as a viable solution. This district provides teachers "with a computer, modem, and software. [The teachers] can take it home so they can develop a high level of expertise. [The district] wants them to be competent computer users so they can transfer their knowledge to the students" (Milone 52).

My own district, I'm happy to say, is following suit. In the fall of 1998, the district implemented the Classroom Technology Integration Program, which is available to all teachers in the district. Any teacher who decides to participate is given a laptop computer. In return, the teacher signs an agreement to do the following:

- attend sixty hours of professional development courses

- use the laptop as an instructional tool
- integrate the technology into the curriculum area
- use the Internet as a research and instructional tool
- use e-mail
- encourage students to use laptops in the classroom and attempt to implement a system of delivering and receiving assignments electronically
- create a minimum of two classroom projects for publication on the district Web site
- work with the onsite instructional technology teacher for professional development

By establishing this Classroom Technology Integration Program, the district sends a clear message about the direction in which it wants to be heading and about the direction in which it wants its teachers to be heading.

Other monies are available as well. Most of it originates at the state or federal level and is earmarked for technology use, dollars often referred to as "use it or lose it" monies. In most cases, the district or the site administration announces that a certain amount of money is available. All teachers need do is apply, usually in the form of a written statement explaining how the technology will be used. In my own case, I wrote two applications for funding and received funding for both. The first proposal earned me a 32" monitor, which I connected to my Macintosh 5200 for classroom display. The second proposal netted me forty DreamWriters.

Portable Word Processors

Several portable word processors are available on the market. The one I am familiar with is the DreamWriter, a small, lightweight word processor manufactured by NTS Computer Systems Company of British Columbia. The particular model I procured (the C200) has a disk drive. I find that with the disk drive I derive valuable use from the DreamWriter; without the disk drive, the DreamWriter would not be worth the cost, even at its lower price.

The DreamWriter has several advantages, the biggest of which is cost. Twenty DreamWriters—together with the cabinet where they are stored, which is conveniently wired for recharging each DreamWriter—cost around $9,000. Subtracting the price of the cabinet leaves a price of about $250 per DreamWriter, about one-fourth the cost of supplying students with laptop computers. This price comparison leads to the logical question: do the extra features and applications of laptop computers make them four times as efficacious as mere word processors? Hardly. Those of us who would like to begin teaching composition by means of word processor but who have not been given carte blanche by our administration would do well to look into the DreamWriter—or any comparable word-processing machine with a floppy disk drive.

Cost, of course, is the major advantage of buying word processors rather than computers. But there are other advantages as well. One is uniformity. Many computer labs lack uniformity. As older computers break down or are phased out, new computers take their places. As a result, many computer labs comprise computers of varying makes and models. Any teacher who wants students to trade disks for the purpose of collaboration or peer review is likely to be inconvenienced by this lack of uniformity. With the DreamWriters, *all* students can open up one another's files without the irksome reformatting that often accompanies moving from one word-processing system to another.

Another advantage is that any classroom can accommodate word processors. Owning a class set means never again having to fight for scheduling time in the computer lab[1] or being held captive to the caprices of the computer lab technician. And not only can the entire cabinet full of word processors fit inconspicuously in any classroom, it does so without the unsightly heaps of wires and cables that are ubiquitous in all computer labs. The inconspicuousness of the portable word processor reaches beyond mere neatness, however. A classroom full of computer workstations shouts, "Computers!" Computers are the focus of that class. Granted, such an environment increases the difficulty of prying students away from their computers for a period of instruction. But with the DreamWriters stored neatly away in a cabinet, the classroom remains primarily a traditional classroom—one that within minutes can be converted into a word-processing lab.

This section is addressed primarily to those who would like to incorporate word processing into their classroom but must do so on a budget. But what of those who intend to purchase computers, not word processors, for their classrooms? An article published in the business section of the *Los Angeles Times*, March 15, 1998 ("Apple," D1) contains data worth considering. The gist of the article is that Apple Computer, long the chief player in the educational market, has for the first time since its inception dropped below 50 percent of the nationwide educational market. For IBM PC users, this news will have no effect on their computer-buying decisions; for Mac users, this news bodes ill. Owning a Mac already brings with it certain inconveniences—the higher cost and the lack of software availability being primary. Up until now, the only place in which owning a Mac was not much of a liability was the classroom. Now, it seems, even that will change. At this juncture, any decision to buy a Mac is a decision based on product loyalty—a decision of heart over mind.

Inservice

> It is imperative that an in-service schedule be set up before teachers are expected to use technology with their students. Using technology in a subject takes time because the instructor must learn how it operates before attention can be turned to thinking about innovative ways to use it. It is generally agreed that depending on the person, mastering a program requires between thirty and fifty hours. (Monroe 75)

Computers bring many changes, and among these changes is the evolution of the inservice. Traditionally, the inservice has been defined as a time for teachers to revitalize their classroom practice with doses of the latest teaching theories and methods. Today, discussions of theory and methodology are taking a backseat to learning technology. One of the negative factors inherent in technology use is the extra time needed for teachers to actually learn the technology. Inservices are fast being converted into technology training sessions as one way to meet the need for extra release time.

In addition to the traditional inservice/technology training session, schools would do well to implement a mentor teacher or buddy system to ensure that the neophytes are not overwhelmed in their attempts to integrate a newly learned technology. Technology mentors are teachers who "are expected to bring what they have learned back to their schools and provide ongoing staff development to their colleagues" (Milone 44). One advantage of utilizing mentors—rather than outside experts—to guide other teachers in technology use is that "teachers in schools with a high level of collegial sharing tend to embrace technology and implement new instructional strategies more quickly" (Sandholtz, Ringstaff, and Dwyer 105).

One example of a successful inservice model is this list of guidelines from the Apple Classrooms of Tomorrow program. Teachers teaching in this program are expected to:

- observe and reflect on a variety of teaching strategies, including direct instruction, team teaching, collaborative learning, project-based learning, and interdisciplinary learning

- engage in hands-on use of computers, productivity software, camcorders, and telecommunications as tools to support learning through composition, collaboration, communication, and guided practice

- interact with students in real classrooms
- share knowledge and experience with colleagues
- create specific plans for technology use in their own classrooms and schools (Sandholtz, Ringstaff, and Dwyer 138–39)

My own district has developed a suitable solution to providing inservice for the district's teachers. Each semester it publishes the Professional Development catalog, a thirty-page listing of training sessions with descriptions of what will be covered at each session. Instructors are teachers from within the district, and training sessions are held either on weekends or after school. To be a presenter at one of these training sessions, all applicants have to do is let the district know that they have an area of expertise and would like to share that expertise. To attend a training session, all applicants need to do is fill out a registration form and mail it to the district office. The district pays all costs. This "teachers teaching teachers" system is an efficient way to provide technology training. It allows each teacher to customize training, and it avoids the high cost of contracting for outside experts.

Among the spring 2001 offerings were sessions on PageMaker, e-mail, HyperStudio, the Internet, Microsoft Word, and Microsoft PowerPoint. Most of these sessions are offered at three levels: beginning, intermediate, and presentation. There was a time when the bulk of the Professional Development catalog was filled with various teaching methodologies; today, the catalog consists of twenty-five pages listing classes on learning computers or how to teach with computers and fewer than five pages on non-technology-related issues.

Summary

This chapter shifted our study of computer-assisted writing instruction from the computers to the composition teachers who will integrate the computers into their classrooms. Placing computers in classrooms will one day be seen as the greatest and most significant decision in modern educational history—or as the greatest of fiascos and an unparalleled waste of money. Decisions made today will determine tomorrow's verdict on the computers-in-schools issue. And the key player in all of this is the classroom teacher. It is the teacher who must decide which practices are best suited to achieving pedagogical aims. And if teachers are to play such a crucial role in the development of computers in the schools, we must take certain steps to help ensure that teachers have the advantages necessary for meeting the new wave of technology. Proper funding, computer availability, and effective inservices are three critical steps.

Practice

4 Teaching Writing with Computers: General Principles

Teachers who decide to transform their composition classrooms from a traditional environment to a computer-based environment should be prepared to make a paradigm shift. The changes teachers will undergo are abundant. Some changes teachers must choose to undergo; others will be dictated by the nature of the computer-based classroom. Chapter 4 examines this paradigm shift in a progression, beginning with some general precepts that will inform a teacher's evolving pedagogy, and moving into a further series of precepts that have components of practical classroom application.

A Catechism I: General Precepts

We must ground all decisions regarding how to teach writing in sound pedagogy, not in the desire to use computers. We must first ask, "What am I trying to do here?" Then ask, "Will technology help me do it better?" (Peckham 337). Computers should be used only "when they in fact aid good classroom practice" (337). Our aim is to "subordinate computer materials . . . to the structure and goals of the class" and to "keep the pedagogy, rather than the computers, in control of the classroom" (Sands 34). Similarly, we must remember that we are teaching composition, not computers (Jewell 54; Sands 33). Ideally, we can teach the technological side of writing with computers "by tightly integrating the introduction of electronic elements with the introduction of rhetorical elements so that teaching, learning, writing and reading remain the focus" (Sands 33).

We must prepare ourselves for "deep, lasting changes in teaching practices" (Cuban, Foreword xiv). Computers themselves are not the equivalent of that change; rather, "technology can serve as a symbol of change, granting teachers a license for experimentation" (Sandholtz, Ringstaff, and Dwyer 171). Ultimately, we will not be able to point to the computers and say, "*There* is change," but to the pedagogies we have developed to better utilize the computers; and these pedagogies should allow both teacher and student to see the production of text in an entirely new and less possessive way, to see text as fluid, temporal, changeable.

And yet, for the sake of self-preservation, we cannot let technology lead the class too far astray from existing curricula. In an ideal world, all teachers would be given license to follow their fancies; but in the present world, "students . . . will be recalled quickly to accepted procedures if standardized test scores fall for the district" (Wresch ix).

To choose computer-assisted writing instruction is to leave behind the comfort and security of those methodologies that have worked for us in the past. It is to gamble for higher stakes: greater successes when our new technology-based procedures work, greater or perhaps more frequent failures when they don't. It is to relinquish a certain measure of control over the results of what we do. It is to incorporate into our pedagogy a tolerance for "acceptable failure" (Williams 43).

The territory we are entering is relatively new. The newness of computer-assisted writing instruction makes experts of us all. We are free from the restraints of relying too heavily on empirical research; instead, we enter into "practitioner inquiry," a mode of inquiry that places "the greatest authority over what constitutes knowledge with the individual practitioner" (Heilker 59).

A Catechism II: Precepts for Classroom Application

We must make students aware of the style-over-substance hazard computers present. Students need to be told—and periodically reminded— that the neatness the computer confers on their work might be wonderful, but it is not to be confused with the content of their writing. The purpose of word-processing features such as spellcheck and font choices is to *support* the text, not to displace it (Takayoshi 249). Our students must maintain vigilance against complacency (Kantrov 70). An occasional exercise in "invisible writing" (turning down the screen resolution so that the writer is forced to concentrate on content only) is one way to focus students on the content of their texts.

We teachers must not become complacent either. When our students first get their hands on computers, we are likely to witness an upsurge in enthusiasm. Lest we become victims of this "novelty effect," we need to employ some or all of the following steps for maintaining interest:

1. Use technology as one tool among many; use computers only when computers are the most *appropriate* tool for completing an assignment, not just because they are available (Sandholtz, Ringstaff, and Dwyer 102–3).

2. Present computers as a component of a larger curricular framework, not as a separate subject unto themselves (Sandholtz, Ringstaff, and Dwyer 102–3).

3. Emphasize the use of general-purpose applications such as word-processing programs as opposed to programmed software that narrows a student's range of choice (Sandholtz, Ringstaff, and Dwyer 102–3).

4. As with individual lessons, the level of computer difficulty must be appropriate for the students, thus avoiding extreme boredom and frustration (Sandholtz, Ringstaff, and Dwyer 102–3).

5. Students must be invested with some of the authority for classroom decisions about how best to use the technology (Sandholtz, Ringstaff, and Dwyer 102–3).

6. If we expect collaboration among our students, we must model collaboration (Kantrov 71).

7. In our stance on the word processor versus pen and paper dichotomy, we must remain flexible. As discussed previously, pen and paper have their time and place. At the same time, we must clear the path for word processing in areas in which word processing was previously not employed—during writing assessments or standardized tests, for example.

This manifesto is offered as a guideline by which teachers might make the transition to a computer-based writing classroom as successful as possible. Having students write on computers will generate an abundance of changes, including entirely new issues that past teachers of composition have not had to explore, or at least not in the same way. Among these issues are classroom authority, revision, gender, cheating, assessment, typing, programmed activities, and immersion.

Loss of Control in the Classroom

The pedagogical changes mentioned up to this point have been recommended changes, those that an instructor would consciously decide to make before taking the necessary steps to produce that change. But teachers who decide to convert to computer-assisted writing instruction should prepare themselves for additional changes that might be forced on them by the technology itself. In "Teaching with Technology or the Technology of Teaching: Reconstructing Authority in the Classroom," Debbie Williams describes a case study of a Web page project gone bad. This project brought to light a previously hidden issue of text ownership. Williams tells of the anxiety she experienced as her role as Unquestionable Authority began to erode and the apprehension that resulted from her "inability to control the logistics of [her] classroom and [her] feelings that [her] students knew more than [she] did" (47).

Teachers who are new to classroom technology use should be prepared for this initial struggle over the loss of authority; but once they work through this initial struggle, benefits will follow. Rick Monroe notes that

> giving up the power associated with being "the one who knows"
> is often the first and most difficult adjustment many teachers have
> to make. After that, everything grows easier. You will find your-
> self changing in subtle but important ways, and you may find teach-
> ing more rewarding because you are talking to students who are
> actively participating in their own learning. (46–47)

Revision-Related Issues in the Classroom

We examine once again our old friend revision. The previous section on
revision was a study of current theories in the nature of revision as it
manifests itself in computer-assisted instruction. This current section
looks at revision through the more practical lens of classroom practice.

The first step in teaching revision is to guide students into an awareness of what authentic revision is and of the ways that computers alter
the nature of revision itself. The computer has obliterated the clear-cut
distinctions between draft 1, draft 2, draft 3, etc. Due to the seamless text
produced on computers, students must relinquish dependence on draft
numbers as indicators of the progress they are making on any given text.

Students must also be guided to an awareness of the distinction
between process and product. In this case, the computer will act as the
teacher's ally. With pen and paper, a student's text will seem productlike
because of the physical nature of the writing on the paper. Not so with
the virtual text that a student generates on the computer screen. The text
is always in the computer, waiting to be tinkered with whenever the
writer desires to do so. Computer-generated text erodes the ground from
beneath the once-solid concept of "finished" text, thus making the
teacher's job that much easier. We simply need to remind students that
the decision to print doesn't mean, "I have finished this text and it is
perfect"; it means nothing more than "I would like a copy at this time"
(Takayoshi 249).

At times the teacher must directly intervene. Ilene Kantrov gives
the example of a student who obsessively tinkers with local revision but
never steps back to consider the overall focus or aim of the text; in this
case, the teacher would need to intervene (67). The teacher should also
intervene in the revision processes of students who do too much or too
little revision. In the latter case, "the teacher needs to be certain that the
student can indeed use the commands for moving and copying text"
(Rodrigues and Rodrigues 17). Elana Joram et al. report that teachers can
often assist advanced writers by instructing them to delay all revision
until a first draft of the text has been generated (189).

Teachers can help their students with revision by apprising them of certain computer-based revision strategies. Possibly the most efficacious among these revision strategies is the hard copy printout (Chandler 198; Kantrov 64, 68). Hard copy printouts can help solve the problem of "disjointed" (Kantrov 68) text that can result from seeing only a small portion of the text on the screen at one time. Chandler suggests that printouts be double spaced, thus allowing the student to annotate with pen between the lines, a type of "interlinear editing" that allows the writer to engage in a "dialogue" with the text (198–99).

Teachers should also instruct students in revising techniques that do not require printouts. Kantrov suggests that to examine text for coherence a "writer can examine just the beginning and end of each paragraph looking for relationships between paragraphs, the logical sequence of ideas, and appropriate use of transitions" (69). In addition to this scrolling technique, writers can use the Find command to search out references to key terms within the text, and use the split screen—if available—to compare one part of a text with another (Kantrov 69).

Gender Issues

The realm of the computer is often considered "masculine space" (Ferganchick-Neufang 15). This perception of computers as the rightful pursuit of men but not of women is pervasive in our schools. According to Mary Ann Zehr, some schools have recognized this gender inequity and are attempting to do something about it. In Beaver Falls, Pennsylvania, computer-proficient high school girls visit the local junior high schools and encourage eighth-grade girls to sign up for the high school's computer program (15). At Parkside Junior High School in Manchester, New Hampshire, a computer-based women's studies course allows girls to gain confidence in their ability to use computers without the sometimes intimidating presence of boys. Since the inception of this program, the percentage of girls in computer classes has risen dramatically, from 12 percent to 30 percent.

As teachers of computer-assisted writing instruction, we are quite possibly helping to alleviate the current gender inequity in computers through the simple act of using computers as writing tools. While it is true that boys have traditionally excelled in the maths and sciences, it is also true that girls are more likely to excel in composition. By uniting composition, an area in which girls are already more proficient, with computers, it seems reasonable to assume that this preexisting skill in composition could lead to better attitudes and increased confidence in the use of computers among girls.

In summary, when we examine computer use among students, we discover a sizable gender gap. As teachers, we can choose to take an active role in diminishing this gap through programs such as those just described. In lieu of the active approach, we might content ourselves with the belief that the simple act of pairing computers and writing will help bring more women into the computer fold. Regardless of where we stand on the issue, all teachers are called on to maintain a sensitivity toward female students in computer-assisted classrooms. As a minority both of general computer users and those in computer careers, they should be given our extra patience and encouragement.[1]

Cheating

Despite the creativity and ingenuity our students apply to the art of cheating, it is unlikely that any student's most enterprising ploy could be called truly original. More than likely, even the most brilliant act of cheating is nothing more than a replica of some previous act of cheating. That is, until the arrival of the computer. The computer has "opened up a whole new realm of student misbehavior," including illegally copying software, protecting disks from teacher access, sabotaging other students' disks, and exchanging online insults with students from other schools (Sandholtz, Ringstaff, and Dwyer 57).

When I began using the DreamWriters, high-tech cheating became an issue in my own classroom. We were using the DreamWriters for class work as well as composition. It occurred to me that one student could easily copy the file of another, thus acquiring a completed assignment without the accompanying drudgery of hand copying another's work. My defense was twofold. First, I revised all assignments to contain at least one item that required a student to answer in his or her own words. Second, I chose a certain item with the potential for a wide variety of student responses and had a student aide copy down the first five words of each response to that item; a quick glance down the list revealed any word-for-word responses. Only once has a student tried the copy-the-entire-file method of cheating. Of course, my students know I am checking, which apparently is deterrent enough.

In addition to offering a wider array of methods for intentional cheating, the computer has also created a variety of more subtle ethical situations. Marcia Halio describes one such situation, in which a student had created a multimedia narration set in an abortion clinic. The narration included actual dialogue from within the abortion clinic. In the background, the shouts of pro-life protesters could be heard. Halio later discovered that the student had had her sorority friends play the part of the pro-lifers by shouting slogans into a microphone. The student made no distinction between real versus staged sounds; in fact, it never occurred to her to do so (345). Ethical? Not ethical?

The computer forces us to define new ethical standards in composition. Students will devise ever more ingenious strategies for intentional cheating and misbehavior, and we will need to develop strategies for catching and circumventing such behavior. In addition, the computer has made the borrowing and integrating of word, sound, and image so easy that we will need to forge new policies regarding plagiarism and ethical standards.

Assessment

The computer has also changed the reading and writing processes at work in the modern classroom. As a result, the pedagogies we employ have changed or are changing. It follows, then, that "if we accept that reading and writing processes are changing as a result of an integral involvement of computers in writing classrooms, then the ways that we evaluate those reading and writing processes will change also" (Takayoshi 253). We can no longer, for example, assess individual drafts; the computer has replaced the draft with a seamless flow of prose. Attempting to assess a student's draft writing is little more than "applying print-based notions of process to computer-assisted writing" (254).

Rick Monroe provides more specific guidelines for assessing electronic prose, calling for two distinct types of assessment: "formative assessment," which determines areas in which the student should endeavor to improve, and "summative assessment," which "brings closure to a piece" (49–50). And it is the portfolio that seems to hold the most promise for the assessment of electronic writing. Because it is a collection of both rough and polished pieces, the portfolio can be used for both formative and summative assessment. All items are appropriate for formative assessment; for summative assessment, students choose those pieces they feel are representative of their best work. The portfolio, then, provides the link between pedagogy and assessment: our pedagogy is the ongoing addition to and improvement of the student portfolio; our assessment is reflected in the student's progress with the portfolio and, ultimately, the improvement and success of the portfolio.

Typing

Better typists are likely to write better than those who possess limited typing skills. Perhaps such an obvious statement is hardly worth making. Yet, in searching the professional journals that address the topic of computer-assisted writing instruction, one might assume that students produce text by means of mental telepathy rather than through manipulation of the keyboard. A preponderance of journal articles are based on the unspoken assumption that all students in a computer-based composition class are more or less equally proficient in typing skill. This, however, is simply not the case. Often the instructor's *first* concern is the range of typing ability within a single class and what to do about those students who can barely type at all.

Rick Monroe is one writer who is aware of the importance of typing ability:

> Our goal is defeated if our students spend twenty minutes pecking out a paragraph on the computer. Even my slowest student can write out a paragraph by hand in less than twenty minutes. . . . If students spend less time editing and writing a clean final draft, they have more thinking time. The ability to use computers as tools can give students a psychological edge as well. Computers can make this one aspect of composing less time-consuming and, therefore, less painful. However, without basic typing skills, say twenty words a minute, we might confound our students. Without realizing it, we might be telling these students they cannot think with either a pencil or a computer. (3–4)

Typing inadequacy does indeed place real constraints on the act of composition. Carolyn Dowling notes that among these restraints are "conscious selection of short words and simple sentence structures, a general tendency toward summary in preference to a fuller exposition of ideas, and conscious rejection of certain character combinations found to be awkward, particularly those involving the outer two fingers" (229). Dowling also points out that in addition to playing an important role in an individual student's composing process, typing is an issue that should be weighted more heavily in our research. Dowling offers Mike Sharples's 1993 study of rhythm in writing (discussed earlier) as an example of a failure to consider typing skill as a significant factor in composition research. In his study, Sharples discusses the writer's natural rhythm of alternating between active composing and passive reflection, declaring that these rhythms are more relaxed and productive for pen-and-paper writers compared to the rhythms of computer writers. Had Sharples compared the rhythms of proficient typists with less proficient typists, he might have made some interesting discoveries that might have altered or further illuminated his initial findings.

As composition instructors, we need to accept the importance of typing ability and apply it to our instruction. If necessary, we might consider having some of our less proficient students spend part of their composition time practicing typing. We might also consider suggesting placement in a typing class, if such placement is feasible. Or we could go beyond the concept of typing skill and teach keyboarding skills as part of our composition classes. Teaching students to become shortcut users rather than mouse-only users, for example, could easily be considered class time well spent.

Immersion

Just as a student's typing proficiency is a variable that must be factored in to both the theory and the practice of teaching composition, the amount of time and the frequency with which a student composes on the computer also play an important part in the overall equation of writing success. Before students are able "to adapt their styles of composing and revising" to the medium of the computer, "students must have on-going access to the computer and sufficient time" (Kantrov 65). Larry Cuban refers to this minimum level of computer access and availability as the "threshold level" (Foreword xiii).

Dawn Rodrigues and Raymond Rodrigues help clarify the concept of computer accessibility by defining three levels: "teaching in a traditional classroom while students have some access to computers in other contexts; teaching in a traditional classroom with regular or occasional use of a computer lab; and teaching in a computerized classroom" (17). Plainly, the highest levels of immersion in composing on computers are more likely to occur in the third category.

Edward Wolfe et al. conducted a study in which "students who [had] no access to computers outside of school received scores almost a full standard deviation lower when their essays were produced with computer" (280). To Wolfe and colleagues, these results lead us to a number of conclusions:

- We will continue to encounter such differences in students' ability to write on computers until we make computers more accessible to all students.
- The lack of computer accessibility results in a lack of "computer facility."
- This lack of facility results in writing that is both inferior in quality and smaller in quantity.

Cindy Sabik asserts that greater immersion in the writing process is one way to combat "the oral habits of an oral culture" (46). According to Sabik, we as composition instructors offer a means of communicating that is superior to orality but that is practiced with such infrequency that many of our students find composing to be fraught with high levels of discomfort. If we truly want to move our students away from habits of orality and into habits of writing, we might follow the lead of those in the foreign language departments. Foreign language teachers have long known that optimum language learning occurs only through immersion, an environment in which only the new language is spoken. If we apply this principle to writing, we and our students would write more and talk less, which means that what was once accomplished through talking should instead be accomplished through writing. Instead of holding a discussion (in which the two or three students who actually read the assigned text do all the talking), have *all* students write responses to the text. To more closely approximate an actual discussion, students can write responses to the first set of responses, ad infinitum. The immersion theory of writing instruction sees its ultimate fruition in online conversation, a mode of conversation in which writing replaces oral conversation entirely.

If we believe that computers should be more accessible to students, then we should take steps to ensure that *all* students have access to computers. Unfortunately, institutional prejudices and blindness have created an environment in which certain groups of students are given priority over other groups. Nancy Traubitz, a teacher at Springbrook High School in Silver Spring, Maryland, tells of her own attempt to create more equitable computer accessibility on her campus. First, Traubitz made the following observations:

> Students in advanced classes had more access to computer equipment at home than students in average classes. Students who had computers available at home used computers more at school. Advanced students liked computers, were comfortable with computers, and used computers more often and in more different ways than average students. (Traubitz 74)

Based on this observation, Traubitz attempted to lead an English class of average-ability students to the same level of comfort and frequency of use as advanced students. In brief, her efforts failed—but not because of the students. Instead of receiving praise for her egalitarian efforts, Traubitz encountered institutional turf wars and narrow-minded entrenchment at each turn. The teachers of advanced classes and computer teachers were the most antagonistic. These teachers felt that the campus's computer labs were theirs by right and that any nontech or nonadvanced class had no right to infringe on their territory. Even within her own department, Traubitz encountered teachers who felt they had a greater right to the computer lab because they were writing teachers and she was an English teacher. Obviously, such divisive attitudes must be identified and overcome. If we truly desire to see students write on computers, then we must include all students in our efforts.

Programmed Activities (Presentation Software)

Assuming you are an instructor with budget money at your disposal (an assumption I do not make), you might be tempted to purchase certain writing or writing instruction software. Save your budget money. The perceived need for such programmed activities is described variously as "an ill-founded hope" (Crafton 322), "counterproductive" (Sands 33), and "a fallacy" (Jewell 54).

Though the aims of those who produce programmed writing activities are worthy ones, the results are inferior to the results of using general-purpose word-processing programs, for several reasons. The use of programmed activities can "easily devolve into teaching students to be users of the software package rather than teaching students to be thinkers who can solve problems in a variety of venues" (Sands 33). Certain features of certain programs—grammar checkers, for instance—are unable to assist a writer with true, holistic revision; instead, these programs "tend to construe revision as error correction" (Crafton 322). Moreover, programmed activities add "an additional layer of complexity to an already complex process" (322), thus creating needless distance between the writer and the writing itself. Finally, since most programmed activities follow some form of the "answer the prompt" formula, students can easily lose sight of the purpose of the program—the writing itself—and see the programmed activity as "an end in itself" (322).

Summary

Change is the one experience common to all teachers who have used computers to transform their classrooms. Adding computers to the writing classroom guarantees a concomitant paradigm shift, which transforms both pedagogy and practice. This chapter attempts to aid the neophyte computer-assisted writing teacher by mapping the inevitable changes. Foremost among these changes are the leaving behind of comfort and security—especially the comfort and security of being the all-knowing authority-in-residence—and the embracing of a pedagogy more open to experimentation. In this new and altered classroom environment, issues such as revision, gender, cheating, and assessment are also altered; by being aware of these alterations, we are better equipped to meet challenges when they arrive.

5 Teaching Writing with Computers: Classroom Activities

The first two chapters of this book discuss the theory that underlies the use of computers to teach writing. Chapter 3 then introduces the teacher as the third point in the composition-computer-teacher pyramid. Chapter 4 examines some of the principles that should define a teacher's approach to computer-assisted writing. Here in Chapter 5, I examine the specifics of classroom practice. Given a classroom full of students and computers, what should the teacher then do? What follows is a compendium of specific lessons and teaching methods.[1]

Sentence Manipulation Activities

Open and Closed Sentence Combining

William Strong (*Creative* 4–5) has created a continuum on which all sentence combining exercises can be placed. At one end of the continuum are "closed" sentence combining exercises; at the other end are "open" exercises. Closed exercises contain more cues and require more specific responses: frequently only one correct response can be given. Open exercises give few or no cues and give the student more flexibility in choice of response. Here's an example of a closed exercise:

> Sentence combining is an approach. (WHILE)
>
> The approach is <u>for teaching</u>.
>
> Some teachers find i̶t̶ useful. (THAT)
>
> Others regard it as dangerous. (Strong, *Creative* 5)

Notice in the closed exercise that the connectives are supplied (*while* and *that*), words to retain are indicated by underlining, and words to delete are marked with strikethrough lines. A correct response to this particular sentence combining problem is: *While sentence combining is an approach for teaching that some teachers find useful, others regard it as dangerous.* Now imagine using a word-processing program to solve this exercise. Some text would be moved, some deleted, some added or altered; and after fine-tuning the spacing and punctuation, the student would have the desired answer. The speed of this process might be called into question, but I don't believe that in this case speed is what matters. Students who use word-processing features to combine the four previous sentences into one single sentence are not only learning to edit with a word processor, but also developing a positive habit that will likely carry over into the editing of their own texts.

Now for a more open activity:

Tirebiter sat at his desk.

His desk was scarred.

He stared at his jogging watch.

It silently ticked off seconds. (Strong, *Creative* 69)

This open exercise refrains from giving the student any information about how the four sentences should be reconstructed. *Tirebiter sat at his scarred desk, staring at his jogging watch as it silently ticked off seconds* is one answer among several. Again, to arrive at this response, a student would use various editing functions, including cutting and pasting the word *scarred.*

Specific-Target Sentence Combining

Specific-target sentence combining focuses on a single component of sentence structure; in addition, the sentences in a specific-target exercise are usually much simpler to combine with a word processor. In this example, the target of the exercise is the participial phrase:

Peter fled from Mr. McGregor. He jumped out a window.

Response: Peter fled from Mr. McGregor, jumping out a window.

In this case, a student would employ a minimum of editing skill to turn the two sentences into the one final response. Notice that in the specific-target exercise, only two sentences are presented; other sentences would only distract the student from the focus skill, which in this case is the participial phrase. In a fuller specific-target exercise, a student would manipulate a series of comparable sentence pairs, each of which would focus on a single skill objective. Other structures that work well in this format are the relative clause, the appositive, the absolute, the adjective phrase, the compound sentence, the subordinate clause, the semicolon, and the run-on sentence. In each case, the exercises can be arranged so that the student simply joins two sentences with a minimal amount of editing.

Text Addition

Text addition requires little or no editing on the student's part. Of the different types of text addition, punctuation is the simplest. A simple drill might consist of five or ten compound sentences that need the comma before the conjunction. A more complex drill (or test) might consist of an entire page of text that requires the student to add a variety of punctuation marks.

Exercises that require students to add words can also be devised. One profitable word-addition exercise asks the student to combine two sentences using a coordinate conjunction, a subordinate conjunction, or a conjunctive adverb. At more basic levels, the student can be supplied with the conjunction; at more advanced levels or at testing levels, the student can be asked to supply the conjunction. For example, the student might be given: *Peter found his jacket. He ran from the garden.* If the student were required to form a compound sentence, he could respond with *Peter found his jacket, and he ran from the garden.* Such a response would require little editing on the student's part.

An exceptional way to teach students the elements of the cumulative sentence is to provide base sentences to which students must add relative clauses, participial phrases, appositives, absolutes, and adjective phrases. An exercise in creating appositives, for example, might consist of five simple sentences. In each sentence, an asterisk represents the position in which the student will create and insert an appositive. For example, a student who is given *Peter's jacket * hung on the scarecrow* might respond with *Peter's jacket, a blue blazer, hung on the scarecrow.* Again, note how this type of exercise is especially suited to the word processor. Students not only augment their skill in the production of appositives, but they are also spared the drudgery of writing out the complete sentences. In addition, students see the production of appositives less as a grammar drill and more as an editing flourish or generative writing tool.

Sentence Modeling

In sentence modeling, the student mimics the structures of professional writers. And just as sentence combining can be understood in the context of a strict-to-loose continuum, so with sentence modeling. Strict sentence modeling requires precise word-by-word replacement. The sentence *Nathaniel dropped his anchor into the sea,* for example, could be modeled as *Bathsheba tossed her television out the window.* In order to produce the modeled sentence, the student must recognize the *noun-verb-possessive pronoun-noun-preposition-article-noun* pattern of the original. This is how modeling works, yet our sample sentences are hardly shining examples of a meaningful modeling activity. Modeling exercises—and, for that matter, any writing exercise—should lead students into producing sentences beyond the range of those sentences they would have produced anyway. The preceding example fails to do this. Consider instead this sentence from C. S. Lewis's *The Screwtape Letters:*

> You no longer need a good book, which he really likes, to keep him from his prayers or his work or his sleep; a column of advertisements in yesterday's paper will do. (55)

To model the C. S. Lewis sentence, students must construct two sentences joined by a semicolon; their first sentence must contain both a nonrestrictive relative clause and a three-item series written as polysyndeton (written with conjunctions instead of commas). The difficulty of the Lewis sentence, however, would make the task of strict, word-for-word modeling too tedious or difficult. This sentence would be better suited for the open, looser approach. If the student were to incorporate the relative clause, the polysyndeton, and the semicolon, all the rest could be approximated. Here's another example of a looser sentence combining activity. The model sentence is from *Among Schoolchildren* by Tracy Kidder (156): *After she let Clarence go, Chris stood at her desk, collecting her homework.*

In a strict modeling format, students would match this ten-word sentence with ten-word sentences of their own. If the class happens to be studying parts of speech, such an approach might be valuable. But in most cases, students are better served by the looser approach to sentence modeling. Loose sentence modeling is more concerned with the larger structures of the sentence; the Kidder sentence, for example, would be seen as an adverbial subordinate clause followed by an independent clause (more simply referred to as a sentence or as the subject and verb) followed by a participial phrase. Though a modeled version of this sentence will follow this same three-part pattern, it needn't be exactly ten words long. By replacing phrases and clauses with like phrases and clauses, the student is freed from the intricacy of word-for-word modeling and is able to learn sentence structure at a more meaningful level.

Once again, we must return our focus to the word processor. Sentence modeling should be considered not just an interesting way to package writing instruction, but also an instructional tool well suited to the word processor. Assuming, for example, that the sentences to be modeled already appear on the screen, students might be asked to replace the original sentence with words, phrases, and clauses of their own. And even if students are simply typing their modeled sentences below or next to the original versions, they'll need to employ an abundance of word-processing skills. Seldom is a student's first modeled version an acceptable one. More often, choices in one part of the sentence will create awkwardness in another part. Much tinkering will be required before an acceptable modeled sentence is constructed, and this is where the editing features of the word processor prove helpful.[2]

Sentence Patterns

Closely related to the sentence modeling approach is another system for teaching sentence construction, known as the sentence pattern. Some common patterns that might be given to students are:

- *Sentence-comma-conjunction-sentence* (for the compound sentence).
- *Subordinate clause-comma-sentence* (for the complex sentence).
- Any sentence that requires the student to embed clauses and phrases: *Subject-absolute-predicate* is one example among many.

Or students can be given patterns in which some of the components are given and others must be supplied by the student. Each of the three previous sentence patterns could also be given as follows:

- In Quebec, Rothschild protested the NAFTA summit, for [ADD A SENTENCE].
- [SUBORDINATE CLAUSE], Mr. Bush invited business leaders from all around the globe to ride roughshod over the environment and all environmental protection standards.
- The well-protected Quebec police department, [ABSOLUTE,] sprayed the crowds with tear gas.

These sentence pattern exercises can be completed in one of two ways: students can either produce their patterned sentences below the originals or replace the original sentence parts with words of their own.

Sentence Options

One of the objects of sentence options activities is to remind students to consider, while they are composing, the several ways an idea might be cast into words. Rather than accepting the first construction that comes to mind, students should savor the available choices and choose the best from among them. Sentence options activities can help students develop this habit.

Here is an example of a sentence options exercise from *Practicing Sentence Options* by William Strong (54):

Basketball Ballet
1.1   The offensive guard is a show-off.
1.2   The show-off is silky-smooth.
1.3   She dribbles the ball.
1.4   The ball is just out of reach.

1A   _____show-off; she_____.
1B   The offensive guard _____ who_____.
1C   _____, a silky-smooth show-off, _____.

This particular sentence options exercise requires the student to construct three versions from the same information. Sentence options exercises are ideally suited for the word processor. The preceding exercise is only a part of the complete exercise. In the complete version, four exercises are given and each is to be written in three ways. That's twelve sentences— and Basketball Ballet happens to be one of the shortest exercises in *Practicing Sentence Options.* The value-to-time ratio (the value of the exercise compared to the amount of time needed to complete the exercise) becomes questionable when students are asked to complete these activities on paper. But with a word processor, students simply replace the blanks with whatever sentence parts are needed to complete the sentences. Not only is the amount of time to complete the exercises greatly reduced, but also students develop proficiency in the art of text editing.

Two Documents, Two Screens

Microsoft Word (and I assume most other word-processing programs) allows the writer to view two documents simultaneously. (Viewing two documents is not the same as the split screen function, which allows the writer to view two parts of the *same* document.) The two-documents, two-screens function allows text to be cut from one screen and pasted into the other. One way for teachers to help students get the most out of this word-processing feature is to assign a two-step essay: step 1, collect the information; step 2, assemble the information. Here is an example of step 1, collecting the information:

Fact Sheet: Whales
- are among the most intelligent animals
- have no ears
- use sound signals to communicate
- use sound signals to navigate
- are the largest living creatures
- strain plankton from the seawater
- are mammals

- can sometimes be found in fresh water
- have voices
- may become extinct
- have teeth
- eat fish . . . (Strong, *Creative* 41)

Fact sheets can be assembled from a variety of sources, but—assuming we are more interested in presenting the student with a focused writing exercise than with a research paper assignment—an encyclopedia will serve admirably. First, students collect their facts and enter them into a word-processing program. (Again, since writing, not research, is the emphasis, the teacher might consider having several fact sheets prepared in advance.) As an optional second step, students might study their lists for similarities between items; by cutting and pasting, similar items can be placed near one another. Now they are ready for a little two-documents, two-screens magic. Students will need to open their fact sheet and then open a new (blank) document. Under Window on the menu bar, click Arrange All. The two screens can be resized for convenience. Now students can produce informational essays by cutting the facts from their fact sheets, pasting them into their essays, and adding some text to flesh out their essays. Rather than worrying about finding information, students can now devote all their energy to the act of writing.

Numerous advantages of the two-documents, two-screens procedure might be listed, but none can compare with its ability to counter the temptations of plagiarism—especially if the teacher prepares a series of fact sheets prior to assigning this activity. In completing this assignment, students have the information they need, but they are not given the sentence or paragraph structures in which to couch the information. In a sense, a level playing field is created, and the resulting essays are products of students' writing abilities, not of their research or plagiarizing abilities.

Text Revision

The teacher needs to prepare text revision exercises. Some examples of text for students to revise are:

- passives, to be rewritten in the active voice
- fragments
- *there is, there are, there was, there were* constructions
- wordiness, to be corrected by omitting needless words
- nonparallel constructions

- inconsistent tense
- generalities, to be corrected by replacing with specific details
- usage errors

Some of these errors—passives and fragments in particular—will be caught by the grammar checker. Consider turning off all grammar checkers before asking students to complete text revision exercises on the word processor.

Beyond the Sentence Level

Most of the suggestions discussed so far are designed for teaching writing at the sentence level. And as a tool for teaching writing at the sentence level, the word processor is unparalleled. But the word processor can be used for instruction at the paragraph and essay levels as well.

Before using the word processor in teaching students the paragraph or the essay, teachers need to construct the exercises themselves. Much like the sentence modeling and sentence pattern exercises described earlier, paragraph and essay activities take the form of templates or scaffolding on which students can build text of their own production.

At the paragraph level, a simple word-processing exercise is to supply students with topic sentences. Students can then flesh out the remainder of the paragraphs by adding support sentences. Conversely, students can be given "headless" paragraphs to which they add topic sentences.

Transitions are a key to cohesive paragraphs. To give students practice in providing transitions, students can be supplied with transitionless paragraphs to which they add transitions. Also, students can be given scrambled paragraphs to rearrange. A paragraph scrambling exercise only works if each sentence in the paragraph contains a transition or some reference to the previous sentence. In the case of highly cohesive paragraphs, students can use the transition signals to reconstruct the paragraph in its original sequence. Again, this makes an ideal word-processing exercise, for a paragraph can be reassembled much more easily through cut and paste than through rewriting.

At the essay level, some of the same principles apply. Perhaps a thesis sentence and some supporting topic sentences can be supplied, thus requiring students to give substance to the supporting details of the essay. Transition practice can be fabricated by requiring students to supply transitions between paragraphs. Finally, practice in writing certain portions of the essay can be provided by leaving out a single paragraph—either the introduction, the conclusion, or one of the supporting paragraphs.

Conventions of the Research Paper

With the many features offered by modern word-processing programs, formatting a research paper—once a near-Herculean task—is within the reach of all students. In this section, we look at two of the requirements of Modern Language Association (MLA) style: the long quotation and the works cited page.

The Long Quotation

MLA style requires that quotations of five or more lines be indented one inch from the left margin. To practice with a long quotation, students need (1) a sentence (or sentences) that introduces the long quotation and (2) the long quotation itself. The simpler the better. You can supply the introductory sentence, the quotation, or both. Since the object of the exercise is to learn the proper formatting, students shouldn't spend too much time gathering the text they will be quoting. The directions might look something like this:

1. Type the introductory sentence. Hit Enter.
2. Type the long quotation.
3. Select the long quotation.
4. Click the Increase Indent button, found on the Formatting toolbar, or use the Control + M shortcut till the long quotation is offset one inch from the left. (Two clicks is the likely number, but the number of clicks will vary depending on the tab settings. Students will know when they've reached one inch of indentation by watching the ruler at the top of the screen.)

Here is an example:

Along the side of U.S. 95 one will find the marker for the Nevada Test Site. It is a simple marker bearing simple words, perhaps an attempt on the part of the U.S. government to conceal some of the consequences of the testing that went on here:

> No one would infer from this marker that nuclear tests detonated here gave leukemia to scores of residents in towns like St. George and Cedar City, Utah, and may be causing the premature deaths from cancer of hundreds more. No one could guess that among the places hit hardest by radiation from this site would be counties in the Midwest and upstate New York. (Loewen 84)

Here are a few more items that pertain to indenting long quotations:

- Do not enclose the quoted material in quotation marks. The one-inch margin indicates that this is quoted material; the quotation marks are therefore redundant.

- For a little extra practice in preparing a research paper, students might be asked to cite the author and page number of the quotation.

- Yes, there is another, more official way to indent text involving the Paragraph dialog box, but the Increase Indent button—or Control + M shortcut—gets the job done in a simpler, more direct fashion.

The Works Cited Page

So that students can focus their practice on actually assembling a works cited page, save them the step of finding sources. Also, by providing students with sources, the teacher is able to control the types of sources that will appear in the works cited page. A few entries will suffice, but choose long entries. Short entries may take up only a single line and thus defeat the purpose of teaching proper formatting. But longer entries will extend two or more lines and give students the proper practice.

You will have to decide for yourself how far into the morass of complexity you wish your students to venture. The *Little, Brown Essential Handbook for Writers* lists fifty-nine different models for making works cited entries, divided into four categories: books, periodicals, electronic sources, and other sources (Aaron 146–47). Since many of these may be used as little as once an epoch, focus on a few simple entries, such as a book with one author, a book with two or three authors, a book with an editor, and an article in a monthly or bimonthly magazine. To save you the trouble of finding your MLA style guide, the formats are listed here:

> A Book with One Author:
> Lastname, Firstname. *Title*. Place of Publication: Publisher's Name, date.
>
> A Book with Two or Three Authors
> Lastname, Firstname, and Firstname Lastname. *Title*. Place of Publication: Publisher's Name, date.
>
> A Book with an Editor:
> Lastname, Firstname, ed. *Title*. Place of Publication: Publisher's Name, date.
>
> An Article in a Monthly or Bimonthly Magazine:
> Lastname, Firstname. "Title of Article." *Name of Magazine* Month. year: starting page-ending page. (The month is abbreviated.)

Once the teacher has decided on the types of sources to include and provided students with a list of sources, the formatting fun begins. As they create a works cited page, students will also learn the importance of setting tabs. And in this case, they learn to use one of the more exotic of the tab settings—the Hanging Indent tab. The first line of a works cited entry begins flush left, but each subsequent line of the same entry is indented a half-inch. No longer must this strange formatting be created through tedious manual manipulation. The Hanging Indent tab now performs the task for us automatically.

There are two methods for setting the Hanging Indent tab:

Method one: First, students must find the little box that sits just left of the ruler. The Left Tab, the one that looks like the letter *L*, is probably pictured in that box. Click away (probably six times) until the Hanging Indent tab is featured. The Hanging Indent tab looks like an upside-down black staple. (While clicking their way to the Hanging Indent tab, students should be encouraged to take note of the tabs they pass on their way, for future reference.)

Once students have clicked their way to the Hanging Indent, they should click on the ruler at the half-inch mark. Of the two sliding pieces that sit at the far left of the ruler, the bottom piece—the one that looks like a little house—should slide over to the half-inch mark where the students clicked. The works cited sources are now ready to be typed in. When students reach the end of line 1, the line 2 text will automatically begin a half-inch from the left margin.

Method two: From the Format menu, open the Paragraph dialog box. Open the Special drop-down menu by clicking on the arrow. Select Hanging. The By window should indicate 0.5" (a half-inch). If not, you can increase or decrease the distance to 0.5" by clicking the up or down arrow. Click OK, and your Hanging Indent is set.

Punctuation and Formatting

Following are exercises for teachers whose students have limited time to spend writing on computers. The drills are not meant to teach punctuation but to familiarize students with the keyboarding aspects of lesser-used punctuation marks. Of course, teaching complete units on punctuation would be superior to the quick lessons outlined below. Each teacher must decide for himself or herself how much time to allot to teaching punctuation in conjunction with computers.

Remember that in all cases, the object is not to teach all there is to know about a certain punctuation mark but to familiarize students with the various punctuation marks found on the keyboard. If nothing else, making students experiment with a lesser-used punctuation mark may give them the initiative to use such lesser-used marks on their own. For a teacher who must go to a computer lab in order to get students in front of computers, time will be limited. In that case, the brief familiarity exercises sketched below will best serve; on the other hand, any teacher with more time to spend with computers should do so.

Italics

Certain features of the word processor are more pleasurable to use than others, and italics must be ranked among the most pleasurable. The italics feature is one of those that make the world of professional publishing more accessible to us mere mortals. Today, when we know that our text will contain a book title, we feel a delicious sense of anticipation, knowing that we will be able to give that book title a professional, italicized appearance. But even today, the underline-titles-of-books rule still lingers in the minds of many students. So we need to be clear: underline when using a pen or pencil; italicize when using a word processor.

Before developing an exercise on using italics, the teacher must first define an objective. If the objective is to teach italics, then the exercise will be longer and will include most or all of the types of word groups that get italicized—titles of books, magazines, music collections; emphasized words; letters or words spoken of as letters or words; foreign words or phrases. But if the objective is simply to acquaint students with or help them develop the habit of using italics, then a few simple sentences with a few book titles will suffice. Students simply find the title, select it, and with a deft Control + I, the title is transformed into an elegantly italicized word group.

Bulleted and Numbered Lists

First of all, students need to be made aware that bulleted and numbered lists are not interchangeable. If the order of the list is pertinent—for example, if the list contains a series of steps that must be followed in order—then a numbered list is called for. If the items in the list can be placed in any order—for example, a list of the eight colors of crayons found in the basic crayon box—then a bulleted list is called for. Of course, the Bullets and Numbering dialog box offers a wide array of bulleting and numbering options, but for the most part, the default setting will see us through any bulleting or numbering task—except for one item. When beginning a bulleted or numbered list, that list will automatically indent a half-inch from the left margin. Quite often this half-inch indentation is what we want. But sometimes—such as when we're making a quiz and we don't want to waste all that space down the left side of the paper—we might not want the half-inch indentation. In this case, after clicking on the bullets or the numbers, click the Decrease Indent button on the

Formatting toolbar, and the list will begin flush with the left margin. Students should be shown this option.

Bulleted and numbered lists can be made up of short, single-word or phrasal items, or they can be made up of complete sentences or multisentence items. In the first type of list, capitalization of the initial letter in each list item is usually called for, even if the items are short. No end punctuation should be used. In the second case, the items are written exactly as if they were contained in a paragraph instead of a list; full punctuation is employed.

As for spacing, in single-spaced text a list is commonly separated from the surrounding text by a double-spaced line (a line of white space). But in text that is already double-spaced, to add any additional white space either before or after a list would create too much space on the page.

Here are a few sample exercises to give students practice with creating bulleted and numbered lists:

1. *Bulleted, short items:* My five favorite animals [or baseball teams or sandwiches or Post-Reformation poets] are as follows:

2. *Numbered, short items:* My five favorite animals, beginning with the most favorite and listed in decreasing order, are as follows:

3. *Bulleted, complete sentences:* To help the reader better understand who Henry David Thoreau was and what he believed, here are five quotations from Thoreau:

4. *Numbered, complete sentences:* To make a delicious cucumber-pepper salad with walnut oil vinaigrette, follow these simple directions:

The Apostrophe

Microsoft Word—and other word-processing programs—will turn your meaningless straight-up-and-down apostrophe into a true curved apostrophe. In order to demonstrate the intricacies of the apostrophe, students will need to see the apostrophes in larger-than-life size. This means using an exceptionally large font on a monitor or screen, or instructing students to use a large font at their own computers.

To familiarize students with the curved apostrophe—used here both as an apostrophe and as a single quotation mark—simply type or have students type the following items:

- doesn't
- Kibbles'n'Bits
- Joe said, "I heard Jim say, 'Never in a million years' to Jane."
- the '60s

Ask students to notice the curves in each of the apostrophes. In *doesn't* and *Kibbles'n'Bits*, the apostrophe is automatically given the correct curvature. In the quotation-within-a-quotation, the single quotation marks are again curved appropriately. But when we reach *the '60s*, we have a problem. Because of the space that precedes *the '60s*, the computer doesn't recognize that the apostrophe is being used to replace the missing *19*.

Here's how students can now fix the mistaken apostrophe. Have them select just the apostrophe. From the Insert menu, choose Symbol. Find the apostrophe that curves in the other direction. (When you've selected it, the words *General Punctuation* will appear in the Subset window.) Now click Insert. Voila! The apostrophe has been fixed.

Brackets

Brackets often come in handy for students writing research papers. Brackets are used to enclose information that appears inside quotation marks but that wasn't actually said by the speaker of the quotation. For example: *"The umpires were blind [this was his favorite excuse] and the manager is a fool,"* *complained Moose.*

Brackets are also used when part of a quotation must be altered for the sake of the reader's clarity. For example, an original quotation reading *John Citizen vowed that he would give him his vote* might be recast with brackets: *John Citizen vowed that he would give [Mr. Nader] his vote.*

The Colon

In case there are still a few souls remaining from the two-spaces-after-a-colon days, remind students that one space follows a colon. Example: *In his pocket, he had the following coins: a penny, a nickel, and a dime.*

The Em Dash

The em dash is so named because it takes up a space close to the width of the letter *M*. This is the real dash, used in such sentences as *Julia Butterfly climbed the redwood tree—the logging companies would not cut the tree as long as she remained there—and began her long sojourn amidst its majestic branches.*

For the bare minimum practice, simply have students create some dashes: *word, hyphen, hyphen, word.* No spaces. The two hyphens do not magically become a dash until a space is added after the word that follows the dash. For this reason, trying to add a dash to preexisting text will require retyping the word after the dash and adding a space.

The En Dash

The en dash—half the length of the em dash but longer than the hyphen—is the correct dash for listing inclusive numbers; for example: *Tonight read pages 12–16.* While an em dash is created by inserting no spaces between the hyphens and the words on each side, the en dash is created by inserting the spaces. Actually, an en dash can be created two ways:

1. *number, space, hyphen, space, number*
2. *number, space, hyphen, hyphen, space, number*

With the first method, the single hyphen will stretch; with the second method, the double hyphen will shrink. And as with the em dash, the computer will not work its formatting magic until you've typed the space after the terminal number. Remind students to remove the spaces around the en dash once it has been created.

Ellipsis

For sheer pleasure in word processing, nothing beats a punctuation mark that magically changes before your eyes. The dash is one such instantly transforming mark; the ellipsis is another. Remember that the word processor considers the ellipsis a single unit, a single space. Ellipsis requires a space on each side, so when demonstrating for students—assuming that the ellipsis occurs in the middle of a sentence—type *word, space, dot, dot, dot, space, word.* As you type the third dot—poof!—the enchantment begins. The dots magically space themselves into a beautiful and professional-looking ellipsis. This automatic spacing, however, is difficult to see in ten- or twelve-point font. To show the ellipsis to its greatest effect, use a much larger font—fill the whole screen if possible.

Creating an exercise that requires students to use the ellipsis is simple. Give students a few sentences that contain a disposable phrase somewhere in the middle. Have students replace the disposable phrase with an ellipsis. Remember that when an ellipsis is placed at the end of the sentence, it is typed *word, space, dot, dot, dot, dot*—three dots for the ellipsis and one for the period.

Consistent Formatting

Punctuation marks generally take the same formatting as the text they are attached to. Consider these sentences:

- In one of Neil Postman's books *(The End of Education),* he claims that our school system promotes several false gods, one of which is technology.

- In one of Neil Postman's books (the 1996 publication *The End of Education*), he claims that our school system promotes several false gods, one of which is technology.

In the first sentence, the italicizing of the parenthetical matter requires the italicizing of both parentheses and of the comma that follows. In the second sentence, the parenthetical matter begins in standard—or roman—font but ends in italics; therefore, both beginning and ending parentheses are set roman—inconsistent with the attached text at the end of the parenthetical phrase but consistent in that both parts of the parenthesis are the same.

When a punctuation mark differs in formatting from the words it is attached to, the result is sometimes a slovenliness of appearance, which can be demonstrated by typing the following in large font for students to see:

- *(slovenly)*
- *(charming)*

In the first example, the parentheses are standard-text parentheses whereas the word is in italics; in the second example, both the parentheses and the word are in italics, thus allowing the parentheses to align themselves with the slant of the word. For the sake of consistency, however, it is conventional to set both ends of the parenthesis in the same font, which is why the closing parenthesis in the second example about Postman's book is set roman rather than italic. If the words next to both beginning and ending parentheses were italic but some of the words in between were roman, both parentheses would be set in italics.

This rule of consistent formatting requires special attention when using brackets, colons, commas, exclamation points, parentheses, question marks, or semicolons.

Punctuation: Summary

The preceding section focuses on those punctuation marks that, due to certain word-processing idiosyncrasies, require students to learn proper word-processing conventions. Hence, certain punctuation marks—the hyphen and the semicolon, for example—are not discussed. As a result, the suggestions in this section are designed primarily to help teachers create word-processing lessons, and only secondarily to help them create punctuation lessons. If, on the other hand, your aim is to teach punctuation, these suggestions can be relegated to a smaller part within a much larger unit.

Other Activities

The Single Monitor/The Data Projector

Throughout this book, all references to writing on computers are based on the assumption that students are doing the writing and that the computers they are using are smaller personal computers. But this is not the only format in which computers can be used to assist in the instruction of writing. The large single monitor and the data projector offer the instructor certain options not offered by a collection of smaller personal computers.

The single monitor is nothing more than a large television screen connected to a computer. The data projector also connects to a computer. With the data projector, the same image that would have appeared on a computer screen is instead projected onto a wall screen. The most salient feature of both the single monitor and the data projector (hereafter, the designation "single monitor" is used to include both the single monitor and the data projector) is the ability of these devices to draw the class together for whole-class instruction. Texts can be displayed on the screen and read by the entire class. The single monitor can approximate the advantages of networking when actual networking is not possible.

The single monitor can be used to show "a videotape of different writers' emerging text" (Rodrigues and Rodrigues 17), and the videotape can be created by "hooking a computer to a videotape machine and recording while someone is writing" (17). Such a recording allows teacher and students to observe how one writer uses the features of word processing to manipulate and edit text while engaged in the act of writing.

The instructor may also use the single monitor to model live writing, a process Mary Schenkenberg describes (3–5). After being handed an extremely poor batch of literary response papers, Schenkenberg decided she could best show her students how to write a literary response paper by having them watch as she composed one of her own. The subject was Faulkner's "A Rose for Emily." As a first step, the class created a list of potential writing topics through a brainstorming activity. After a good deal of paring down, the students selected Emily and her relationship to the old South as the topic. Then a thesis statement was devised: "In 'A Rose for Emily' by William Faulkner, Miss Emily represents the fall of the old South." A second brainstorming activity ensued in which the students listed the various similarities between Emily and the old South. With a thesis statement and a list of supporting ideas in her arsenal, Schenkenberg proceeded to write the essay. This live modeling method of teaching has numerous advantages over other methods. Perhaps the greatest is the potential of leading students to the epiphany, "Hey, that's not so hard. I can do that too."

Rick Monroe provides another example of using the single monitor to provide writing instruction (24–25). Before asking his students to complete an exercise in poetry modeling (using the same phrasal structure or parts of speech as a professional model but supplying words of their own), Monroe decided to model the activity for the class using the split screen function available on most word-processing programs. On the top portion of the screen, Monroe displayed the original poem. On the bottom portion of the screen, Monroe created his modeled version of the original, explaining his thought processes as he wrote.

During the 1997–98 school year, I had my first experience with using a 32" monitor, which I connected to a Macintosh 5200 computer. My experience was notably positive, though I did discover two drawbacks to teaching with a monitor. First, from my position behind the computer, I could see only half the class. To address students who sat in the eclipsed portion of the classroom, I had to lean over and peek around the monitor. This problem, however, is easily solved by substituting a laptop for the full-sized computer. The other problem with the single monitor is that students in the back row are unable to read the print unless the font is extremely large. In my own classroom, students could comfortably read the screen when the font was increased to 36-point. This means that frequently only one sentence appears on the monitor at one time.

Despite these inconveniences, I find the single monitor a worthy tool. It focuses student attention, and it allows students to observe the ways in which an "expert" uses a computer to manipulate text, whatever lesson or skill one might be trying to teach. The MacAcademy, a company that provides computer instruction through seminars, teaches computers this way; seminar participants watch a projection screen as the instructor demonstrates various computer techniques.

Spellcheckers and Grammar/Usage/Style Checkers

Today, all word-processing programs come equipped with a spellchecker program; many come with grammar or usage checker programs as well. Inherent in such programs are advantages as well as certain disadvantages, and we would do well to acquaint ourselves with both sides of the issue before making any decisions about how we or our students will use spellcheck or usage check programs in the classroom.

Timothy Beals, in response to a journal article comparing the "calm, reasonable" responses of computers with the "hostility and mean-spiritedness" (67) of many teachers' responses to student writing, decided to perform his own analysis of Editor, a "sophisticated grammar and style checker" (67). Beals submitted two short essays for the style checker's approval, and the style checker responded by pointing out eight errors of word choice or punctuation. In all eight cases, the writer was correct and the style checker was wrong. In almost all of the eight cases, it was the style checker's inability to understand the context of the writer's choices that led to its incorrectly identifying the eight "errors."

Of course, we've known since the inception of the first writing aids that their ability to help writers is limited. The dictionary provides us with the most common example of this truth: dictionaries are helpful only to those with reasonably sound spelling skills. To the person who has little clue how a word is spelled, a search through the dictionary will likely end in frustration.

I've seen this principle in effect with my own students in their attempts to use spellcheckers and grammar checkers. When a word is designated as misspelled, a good speller will recognize the correctly spelled word from among the suggestions offered by the spellchecker. When the grammar checker flags grammar-related problems, those who have a solid understanding of typing conventions and the structure of the English language will know how to fix the problem. But many students who do not possess a sufficient level of expertise in spelling or grammar are only bewildered by the computer's suggestions.

Another drawback to spellcheckers and grammar checkers is students' tendency to let the spellchecker and grammar checker replace the effort involved in rereading the text. A student who, on finishing the checking of a document, heads straight for the printer may well have produced more errors—and more egregious errors—than the student who simply reread his or her text.

Nevertheless, I find that the spellcheckers and grammar checkers are valuable tools because they at least say to the student, "Something may be wrong here. Let's stop to think about it." What this translates into in the real-life classroom is a plethora of students asking the teacher to show them what must be done to fix the flagged error. Paradoxically, since my students began using the DreamWriters, which have spellcheckers, the number of times I hear "Mr. Moeller, how do you spell this word?" has increased fivefold. And, as long as the teacher has the energy and the inclination to play dictionary-in-residence, this is not an undesirable state of affairs.

I've found that the built-in checkers offer other advantages as well. They catch much of the minutiae that, due to the constraints of time, teachers must often allow to pass unnoticed. Spacing conventions such as "no space to the left of a comma" and minor irritations such as the ubiquitous "alot," for example, are caught by the grammar and spellcheckers, thus freeing us to attend to more important issues such as substance and coherence. Conversely, the grammar checker can at times become a hindrance, especially when the checker, for whatever reason, reports an error that is not an error. Better writers have the confidence to skip the computer's suggestion and go on, but less competent writers treat the computer's suggestion like a police tape—they refuse to cross. Instead, they ask the teacher for advice. The result is that an undue portion of the teacher's time is spent walking to students' desks and saying, "Just skip it."

Of course, if we really want a usage checker to flag only those constructions we want flagged, we should customize it. Edward Klonoski describes how students can use the search or find functions present in all modern-day word-processing programs to search for constructions chosen by the teacher. Klonoski (76) offers the following sampling of constructions that students might be instructed to look for:

It, This, There	indefinite pronouns and "to be" verb
You/your	avoid this voice
I think/I feel	consider deleting
by	accompanies the passive voice
fact, reason	empty expressions
like	check if *similar to* works
very	weak modifier
tion, sion, ment, ance, ence	nominalizations
it's	see if *it is* works
'	eliminate contractions,
'	check possessives
not un	double negative
in today's society	substitute *today*
being	consider deleting

Also consider searching for pronouns, especially *he;* negative words such as *not* and *never;* commas; and semicolons.

Klonoski is quick to point out that instructing students to run a personalized search program will be futile unless students are familiar with each of the items on the search list. Students must understand *why* the listed constructions are inferior and what options are available for amending them. Only after the instructional foundation has been laid will students understand "which constructions they misuse and which do not pose a problem" (Klonoski 76).

The Portfolio

Throughout the semester, students will produce a variety of texts. The portfolio can serve as a framework for these texts. Typically, the portfolio is a collection of a student's writing throughout the semester. The teacher might provide a checklist that outlines the minimum requirements for the portfolio. In addition, students are frequently asked to survey their semester-long writing production and evaluate both their own proficiency and the amount of progress they have made.

The computer is well suited for generating portfolios. Because students continue to save their writing—probably to a floppy disk—as they progress, the production of a portfolio is inherent in the act of writing on a computer.

Sequencing is one key to a well-formulated portfolio. Assignments might be sequenced "from the more personal to the more academic" (Sands 34) while simultaneously being sequenced to incorporate "a variety of appropriate emerging technologies" (33). In other words, assignments should build not only on previously learned writing skills, but on previously learned computer skills as well.

Read-Arounds

The typical read-around session usually follows this procedure: First the class is divided into small groups. Then papers are divided into subsets and distributed. All the members of a group read all the papers within a subset by reading a paper and passing it on. Often the group discusses each paper for the purpose of adding comments or scores.

The electronic read-around (Jewell 56; Monroe 7) follows much the same script. But instead of trading papers, students trade computer screens by trading seats. At each new computer screen, students are able to add comments. Peer comments can be distinguished from the original writing by having commentators cast their comments in a different font, a different color, or in all caps.

With the DreamWriters, I devised a system that allowed students to read one another's papers without having to change seats. First, I took all the floppy disks for a particular class and divided them into random piles (more piles if you want students to read only a few papers; fewer piles if you want students to read more papers). I then combined all the writing files contained within each stack of disks and combined these files into a single file. Finally, I copied this group file back onto each disk. Each student's disk now contained a sampling of other students' texts. Merely by scrolling down, students were able to read their classmates' writing as they wrote their peer responses on separate paper.

Publishing and Audience

By ensuring that student papers will be read by other students, the teacher assists the student writer by creating a more specific sense of audience. Through publishing, a teacher can harness this same sense of audience and raise it another level. Of course, the teacher can always encourage out-of-school publishing by posting contest entry forms or having students search books such as *The Market Guide for Young Writers* (Henderson). But, realistically, only our more proficient students are likely to find success in getting their writing published.

What of the rest of our students? They too can see their work in print, thanks to the computer. The computer has taken the once tedious task of assembling a classroom magazine and made it the most elementary of tasks. Word-processing or desktop publishing programs will give the classroom magazine a polished, professional look. Formatting the text in two or three columns will provide a more magazinelike look. Through programs such as ClarisWorks, Microsoft Works, or Print Shop, art and graphics can be easily imported. Forty-pound paper stock can serve as the front and back cover, and three-ring binders or staples and tape are two inexpensive, workaday solutions to the binding problem.

Through the classroom magazine, many students will experience the pride of seeing their work in print. To further capitalize on students' pride in their writing and in their magazine, consider distributing the classroom magazine beyond the confines of the school. Copies can be distributed to administrators, school board members, district school libraries, local public libraries, doctors' offices, realtors' offices, and the waiting room at the local hospital (Worman 48).

Collaborative Writing

Richard Jewell's method for using computers as the basis of collaborative writing is quite similar to the read-around described earlier. It involves students moving from one computer to another, but instead of commenting on the writing of another, students add "a sentence or two" (56) to the text that appears before them. Although this activity works well in either the narrative or the essay form, Jewell claims that it works especially well with argumentative writing: students are forced to decide what statement would logically follow from what has come before. At times, Jewell is even more specific, asking

> each student to type a one-sentence opinion or belief, then move to the next computer and add a supporting reason for the argument then facing him or her, moving again and adding an explanatory sentence, then an imaginary quotation, then a statement of the quotation's implications, then a specific example, then a new supporting reason or perhaps an opposing viewpoint, etc. (56)

Joan Hamilton offers an interesting variation on the collaborative writing process (66–70). Using the poetry of "Song of Myself" as a model, the class produces a single poem that includes lines from all class members. Key lines are chosen from Whitman's original poem. The beginnings of the lines are retained, while students add their own conclusions to Whitman's beginnings. Lines such as "I think I will listen . . ." and "I understand . . ." and "I stand in a meadow and look . . ." are examples of lines that lend themselves to thoughtful completion.

Once the students have written their own versions of the Whitman lines, they assemble the lines into a single poem. Hamilton arranges the final version of the group poem with the original Whitman phrase flush left, with the ellipsis. Student additions are then added vertically in list form. To keep the poem within an acceptable length, the class must decide democratically which lines are worthy of being included in the class poem.

Invisible Writing

Invisible writing involves simply turning down the resolution on the screen until it is dark (or the text is no longer seen) and then typing. This prewriting activity is designed to help writers focus on text production and text production only. While in the invisible writing mode, students are "freed from the compulsion to spend their time doing 'local editing,' fixing trivial typing errors, or making relatively minor changes in the text at the expense of the broader ideas they are trying to articulate" (Marcus 12).

Lesson Files

To this point, all that has been said about using computers in the classroom has been based on the assumption that students will be using the computers to compose—to generate essays or narratives. But composing is not the only activity that takes place in the classroom. Even in a composition class, students will engage in exercises designed to improve their composition skills. Just as students use the computer to compose texts, so can they use the computer to complete writing exercises.

Frequently, the computer can take the tedium out of textbook exercises, thus making them more valuable. For instance, consider a grammar book exercise that asks students to correctly punctuate compound sentences. There was a time when students had to copy out the sentences before placing the comma in front of the conjunction. It might take half an hour to cover ten to fifteen examples. But with the computer, the same benefit can be derived in five minutes. True, the workbook also offers the same advantage, but the workbook is disposable; with the computer, no trees are killed.

When incorporating writing exercises into computer files, look for exercises that are tailor-made for the computer. Sentence combining exercises are a good example. With sentence combining, the student can combine sentences by using word-processing features such as cut-and-paste instead of copying out the entire sentence. The computer "shifts the students' focus from the physical burdens of writing and their fears about the permanence of what they are putting down, to what they think about a topic and have to say about it" (Schipke 87). The result is that students derive the intended benefit of the sentence combining exercise as well as the additional benefit of increased facility with text manipulation.

Another advantage of the lesson file is its capacity to individualize instruction. One way to individualize instruction is to arrange files by level of difficulty; another method is to designate certain files as extra credit files. Either way, you achieve the same end. Basic writers can work at their own speed on exercises at their own comfort level, and more proficient students can work ahead without wasted instructional time. When they finish one file, students simply open another of their choice.

Following is a list of various exercises worth being converted into lesson files. Each of these exercises has been chosen on the basis of two criteria: (1) it teaches a worthwhile writing skill and (2) it is computer-friendly. Because the basis for each item's inclusion has already been explained, each item is listed with a minimum of explanation. It is enough to have the kernel of each idea; from this kernel, teachers can construct lesson files based on their own preferences and examples.

- Responding to literature prompts. Such prompts placed on lesson files can replace the standard book report. Lists of such prompts can be found in *Writing and Thinking with Computers* by Rick Monroe, pp.100–101, and "Fifty Alternatives to the Book

Report" by Diana Mitchell in the January (vol. 87) 1998 *English Journal*, pp. 92–95.

- A list of journal writing topics.
- A variety of creative writing prompts.
- Replacement activities. Any assignment that asks the student to replace weak or ill-chosen words with better words (e.g., replacing the verb *get* or the verb *to be*).
- Movement activities. Create a list of sentences that contain movable parts. For example, students can be instructed to move participial phrases from the beginnings to the ends of sentences. This exercise makes particularly good use of the cut-and-paste function. It also compels students to discover some of the rules of punctuation.

These are just a few ideas for lesson files; this list is not intended to be exhaustive or prescriptive. Lesson files are the business of the individual teacher. Almost any favorite lesson will work well as a lesson file as long as teachers keep this important requirement in mind: the lesson should be easier to complete on computer than with pen and paper; otherwise, the purpose of the lesson file is defeated.

Whole-Class Lessons

Lesson files are intended for individual instruction. But numerous whole-class lessons are also well suited for computer-assisted writing instruction. Following is a listing of such lessons offered by teachers who have had success with them.

The collaborative story between classes (Monroe 35–37). The collaborative story, which was briefly described earlier, can also be extended between classes, thus breaking down the barriers of grade and age. Assuming a teacher has five classes, students in the first period each write one-fifth of a narrative; students in the next class write the next fifth, and so on. The organization of such a project—e.g., giving credit, shuffling floppy disks—will require some ingenuity on the part of the instructor. In fact, a clever scheme of organization is vital to many of the assignments in this section. But because different teachers will be working under different technological circumstances, each teacher will have to decide on the organizational plan that works best for her or him.

The minidictionary (Neumann 14–16). This activity is recommended for use with lesser-motivated students. First, students brainstorm a list of topics that might interest them. Then they choose a topic and research that topic. On the computer, students compose a dictionary of terms that relate to that topic. When finished with the dictionary, they compose a one-page accompaniment to their dictionary in which they discuss their topic, what they learned about it, and how they rate their own work on the project.

Creating short fiction from eight words (Heyn 32–34). Students begin with four pairs of words as the bare bones of a short piece of fiction: *He left. She laughed. Their loft. That's life.* Here are the steps:

1. Replace the pronouns with proper nouns.
2. Build up the first three word pairs with prepositional phrases or initial verbal phrases built on the original verb—or create a new subject and verb while turning the original word pair into part of a dependent clause.
3. Change the order of the sentences by moving at least one of them.
4. Insert linking words or transitions.
5. Add details and, if so desired, dialogue.
6. Do any other revision or editing you deem appropriate.

The diamond poem. The object is to write a narrative poem, usually a dialogue consisting of alternating quotations, in the shape of a diamond. Instructions can be precise—line 1, one word; line 2, two words, and so on—or allow for approximations of the word count as long as the resulting poem is something akin to the shape of a diamond. This poetic form is ideal for the computer. In order to achieve the diamond shape, students must use the center text function as they type. Double spacing also helps.

Poetry with graphic highlights (Hackett 49–53). To begin with, students write a poem, any poem. Hackett suggests that less-accomplished writers try the cinquain. The graphics are added in two stages. First, students search their poems for words that can be highlighted or accentuated by means of the word-processing program itself, choices such as font size, font style, boldface, shadow, etc. Once this preliminary stage has been concluded, students access a graphics or clip-art program. They choose a few key graphic elements that are significant within the context of their poems.

The manual for parents (Trimble 54–58). Students create a booklet based on the theme of parenting. The booklet contains the following elements:

- A cover, including a title, the student's name, and some original art using a draw program
- A dedication page that includes a documented quotation
- A "do's for parents" list

- A "don'ts for parents" list
- A sketch of the ideal parent, using a draw program, with an explanatory caption
- A sketch of a real parent, using a draw program, with an explanatory caption
- A composition describing an important childhood memory
- A description of the student's fictional child or children

The autobiographical newspaper (Morics 109–12). To complete this project, students must have access to a publishing program that allows them to format text in columns, create newspaperlike headlines across columns, and add graphics. If such a program is not available, using the column feature available in most word-processing programs is the next best choice.

Students first complete an autobiographical questionnaire, preferably with the help of parents. Using this completed questionnaire as a source, students create newspaperlike accounts chronicling the major events of their lives. Finally, by adding headlines and graphics, clip art, and/or draw program photographs, students construct their autobiographical newspaper.

Using Word-Processing Features

Certain features of the word processor can be harnessed to emphasize specific instruction rationales. Formatting features such as bold, italics, underlining, color, and highlighting, for example, can be used in any exercise that requires students to find certain words or phrases. In a subject-verb exercise, for instance, subjects can be boldfaced and verbs can be underlined. Students can turn all subordinate clauses red; figurative language can be italicized; items in a series can be underlined; a series of parallel sentences connected by semicolons can be highlighted. The possibilities are endless.

Transferring Assignments Electronically

In a networked school (a school in which every computer is hooked up to every other computer), each teacher and student can have a folder of his or her own. On the student server, a shared folder can be created into which students can drop papers. Teachers can grade these papers and then return them by dropping them back into the student's folder. This method works much better than sending papers through e-mail. The e-mail method requires the teacher to save each document, which the student usually sends as an attachment, and to resend it by e-mail once it has been graded. Two other problems with the e-mail method include: (1) Frequently the student's original formatting will become altered, leaving the teacher with Martian-like documents to grade. Students must learn to send documents in plain text format. (2) Students must include error-free e-mail addresses on their documents; otherwise, the teacher will not be able to return them.

Teachers in non-networked schools might consider accessing blackboard.com. This is a free Web site that allows teachers to create classes on the Internet. First the teacher creates the class. Students log into the class; part of the process requires them to enter their e-mail addresses. The class Web site has a drop box into which students upload their papers. When the teacher logs in, he or she sees the student papers in the drop box. The teacher grades them and then clicks Send, and the program automatically sends the papers back to the students. It knows the e-mail addresses, so the teacher doesn't have to.

Checking Student Work

The first question to ask when deciding whether to use the word processor for a writing exercise is: "Does the word processor offer any advantages over completing the same exercise with pen and paper?" In the case of those exercises listed earlier—and probably in many other exercises as well—the answer is yes. But before we decide to commit our entire repertoire of writing exercises to disk, consider the end result—students printing their work. Imagine a simple activity such as taking ten sentence fragments and correcting them. "OK. Everyone done? Now let's all print." Not such a pleasant thought. Even if students work at home and bring their work to class, that doesn't alter the reality that printing from a computer is more resource intensive than using pen and paper: paper plus printer cartridge plus electricity is more wasteful than paper alone. True, for some assignments—a final copy of an essay, for example—a printed hard copy might be indispensable. But for class work, we need to be resourceful about discovering ways to check or give credit for student work without that work being sent through the printer. Font size, font style, font color, and pop-up notes are a few of the devices we have available for commenting on student papers.

Teaching Word Processing and Keyboarding

Some researchers warn against allowing the composition classroom to become a computer classroom; others, such as Rick Monroe (78–82), prescribe a sequential program of teaching word processing. My own opinion is that writing and word processing are so indissolubly linked that to teach word processing *is* to teach writing.

The primary requirement for whole-class word-processing instruction is that the instructor and each of the students use the same word-processing program. Ideally, the instructor would be able to demonstrate word processing by means of the single monitor or the data projector, but this not essential.

As for the best method for teaching word processing, let the program itself be your guide. First, dictate a few sentences of text to the class. (I use a seven-sentence impromptu version of "The Three Little Pigs.") Incorporate a few errors into the text for the sake of later manipulation. Then go to the menu bar. Working from left to right, explain or use each function on each of the pull-down menus. After each demonstration of a menu bar function, have students practice the same maneuver using the keyboard shortcut. Stress the importance of these shortcuts and that using the shortcut is preferable to using the menu bar. Included in a student's repertoire of shortcuts should be the mouse-click method of selecting text by clicking on that text. Finally, explain or use any other function found elsewhere on the computer screen. The little pop-up boxes that appear when students hold their arrows over different icons will assist teacher and students as they navigate the computer screen. By using this simple method, a teacher can thoroughly cover the entire range of functions offered by the word-processing program without having to spend any time in planning.

What to Teach

The following lists are offered as aids for teachers planning a unit on using the word processor.

Skills and Functions to Teach—More Essential and Basic

- Alignment (left, center, right, justified)
- Columns
- Copy and paste (and the Clipboard)
- Cut and paste (and the Clipboard)
- Find, Find and Replace
- Font (and font size)
- Help
- Line spacing (especially Control + 1 and Control + 2)
- Minimize and restore
- Moving around the screen: includes moving while moving text,

moving without moving text, and cursor keys (home, end, page up, page down)

- Page Setup
- Print Preview
- Printing (the choices available within the Print dialog box)
- Right clicking
- Save (difference between save and save as; also the difference between saving to drive C (at home this is usually the My Documents folder) and saving to a disk
- Scroll bars
- Selecting and Deselecting Text
- Spellcheck, grammar check
- Thesaurus
- Toolbar buttons (how to show or hide buttons)
- Undo
- Using tabs
- Views (normal, Web layout, print, outline)

Skills and Functions to Teach—More Advanced

- AutoCorrect (how it works and how it can be modified through the AutoCorrect dialog box)
- AutoFormat (how it works and how it can be modified through the AutoFormat dialog box)
- AutoSave (make sure it's on)
- Footnotes
- Hanging indent
- Indenting (via the Format Paragraph dialog box, in addition to the Tab key)
- Numbering pages (automatic and headers/footers)
- Outlining
- Sort (to alphabetize lists)
- Split screen
- Symbols (to insert)
- Word count

Afterword: *Verbum Sapiendi*

In a relatively brief period, the personal computer has gone from inconceivable dream to vital component in homes and schools throughout the world. The ubiquitous presence of computers is still a new phenomenon, especially in the writing classroom. As teachers of computer-assisted writing instruction, we are pioneers. The field is still in its infant stages, and decisions we make now will have ramifications many years from now.

This book focuses on the connections between computers and composition—composition, that is, as we know it in the traditional sense. But this is only a start. There are other computer-related writing domains not discussed in this book, domains that are likely to grow more significant in future years. E-mail, networking, online communication, multimedia, Web pages, hypertext—these are just a few of the communication-related phenomena that computers make possible and that may prove to be the essentials of tomorrow's writing classes.

We should be enthusiastic about the yet-to-be-tapped potential of using computers to teach writing. Only a few short years ago computers were seen as a tool for allowing students to complete grammar drills at an individual pace—the computer as a replacement for teachers. Already our vision of what the computer can do in the writing classroom has broadened considerably. We have recognized that we are teaching more than just writing; we "are teaching a new way of thinking about and working with writing—a way of thinking of text as fluid and movable, a way of thinking about communication as dynamic and purposeful" (Rodrigues and Rodrigues 23). And in the years ahead, we may come to perceive of writing in ways undreamed of by today's most progressive researchers.

But a desirable transformation will not come about on its own. It is up to classroom teachers—those in the trenches—to take a proactive approach to computer-assisted writing instruction; yet, at the same time, teachers must remain focused on the ends of their instruction. We must avoid beginning with the computer and then pondering how to use it; instead, we must clearly define our goals—improved writing and communication skills—and then discover how the computer can best help

---

The appendix title means "a word to the wise."

us achieve those goals. For many, these will include the goals of constructivist pedagogy—democratization, collaboration, small groups—and for others these goals will include the more traditional aims of the teacher-as-repository-of-knowledge.

The key to discovering those uses for which computers are best suited is a breadth of knowledge and experience. The primary goal of this book is to provide that breadth of knowledge for the neophyte instructor. Another goal is to encourage a well-balanced attitude toward the computer—neither the starry-eyed optimism of the techno-reformer nor the closed-mindedness of the Luddite. Computers have their place, but that place is not everywhere; computers are a laudable tool, but they cannot take the place of a warm-bodied human being—the teacher.

The Middle Road

Without question, techno-reformers have accomplished a prodigious amount during the past decade. Expenditures for technology in education will exceed $10 billion in the year 2001. Virtually every school in the country now owns computers; the ratio of kids to machines has been steadily dropping and now averages 10:1. Two-thirds of schools have access to the Internet and three-quarters have cable television (Wolk 3).

They're here. Computers—with all their technological accoutrements—are arriving at campuses all across the country. And once the computers arrive, teachers will have decisions to make. Not *Do I or do I not make use of computers?*—*that* decision has already been made. The computers *will* be used. Administrators are already building the "uses technology" language into teacher evaluation documents. Today, instead of deciding *if* they will use computers, teachers will be deciding *how* to use computers.

For teachers, an informed decision will avoid the two extremes—on the one hand, blind acceptance; on the other hand, blind rejection. Identifying a middle way between these two extremes is one of the objectives of this book. In addition to exploring this middle way, teachers should:

- turn a critical eye toward our brave new technology-enhanced classrooms
- endeavor to understand the evolution of computer-assisted writing instruction over the course of its brief history
- survey controversial issues and current theory in the field of computer-assisted writing instruction
- explore the advantages and disadvantages of using computers to teach writing

- examine the role of the teacher as the cornerstone of all computer-assisted writing instruction and devise various methods for teachers to access and utilize technology to teach writing

The ranks of technology-wielding writing teachers should be filled with well-rounded individuals, instructors who can trace the development of computer-assisted writing and who see how the discipline got to where it is today; who are aware of the negative as well as the positive research in the field and who thus avoid attempting to use technology in unfruitful ways; who are grounded in both sides of the discipline's controversies and thus are more likely to present well-balanced instruction; and, most of all, who are enthusiastic about the possibilities offered us by linking technology with writing instruction.

Drawbacks to Computers

Today, the enthusiasm with which we stock our campuses with technology exceeds the enthusiasm with which the residents of Troy hauled the wooden horse inside their walls. Judging by the pro-technology cheerleading one hears during inservices or the omnipresent administration-penned memos that fill one's mailbox, teachers should get behind this technology-bearing wooden horse and push even harder. Only when one turns to the professional—and some popular—journals does one hear the suggestion that maybe we should check for Greeks. Even those of us who have already chosen to embrace computers in the classroom should be aware of opposing viewpoints.[1] Opposing viewpoints can remind us that the computer is only one choice among many, or in the words of Lowell Monke, "When we consider using computer technology, we [should] think about what will be lost as much as we think about what will be gained" ("Web and the Plow" 32).

The most general, and perhaps best-known, objection to the computer comes from Wendell Berry's "Why I Am Not Going to Buy a Computer." He begins his essay with the following manifesto:

- The new tool should be cheaper than the one it replaces.
- It should be at least as small in scale as the one it replaces.
- It should do work that is clearly and demonstrably better than the one it replaces.
- It should use less energy than the one it replaces.
- If possible, it should use some form of solar energy, such as that of the body.
- It should be repairable by a person of ordinary intelligence, provided that he or she has the necessary tools.

- It should be purchasable and repairable as near to home as possible.

- It should come from a small, privately owned shop or store that will take it back for maintenance and repair.

- It should not replace or disrupt anything good that already exists, and this includes family and community relationships. (Berry 171–72)

Another "techno-skeptic" is Stanford education professor Larry Cuban, who in his 1997 *Los Angeles Times* editorial ("Unless Teachers" M1) questions the "river of technology dollars . . . flowing through the nation's schools" and the "oft-repeated claim that computers produce better-educated kids." Cuban notes a loss of "direct experience and social relationships," especially during early childhood. Cuban also discusses "uneven access" to computers, with "affluent, white, English-speaking students use[ing] computers more than their less affluent, nonwhite, nonnative-speaking peers" (*Teaching* xi).

In the October 1997 issue of *Teacher Magazine,* Lowell Monke bemoans the loss of many of our humanist values, a loss he believes is tied to the advent of the computer. With the ubiquitous presence of the computer,

> there seems to be a substitute for each of these [human goals]: for the pursuit of truth, the pursuit of skills; for the comprehension of great ideas, the compilation of them; for the generation of one's own ideas, the slick packaging of others'; for the discovery of meaning, the search for resources; for the use of good judgment, reliance on data analysis; for the exercise of emotional maturity, the diminished challenge of disembodied relationships; for the development of wisdom, the achievement of success. ("Web and the Plow" 33)

In his July 1997 cover article for the *Atlantic Monthly,* Todd Oppenheimer turns a critical eye toward the computer revolution. Among Oppenheimer's objections are the following:

- The cost: "between $40 billion and $100 billion" federal dollars over the next five years (45).

- The displacement of traditional subjects: "U.S. teachers ranked computer skills and media technology as more 'essential' than the study of European history, biology, chemistry, and physics . . . and than reading modern American writers such as Steinbeck and Hemingway or classic ones such as Plato and Shakespeare" (46).

- The schools' loss of autonomy to the business sector: "if business gains too much influence over the curriculum, the schools can become a kind of corporate training center—largely at taxpayer expense" (55).

- The "ill informed, or just superficial" information that students imbibe, uncritically, from the Internet (61).
- The danger computers pose to our children's already tenuous reading skills.
- Online conversations and the resulting loss of "the unpredictability and richness that occur in face-to-face discussions" (62).

Each of these challenges to our uncritical acceptance of computers in the classrooms is a valid one. We need to think deeply about the directions our digital classrooms might be leading us. Yet, if there is one domain of computer usage most exempt from the foregoing criticisms, that domain would have to be computer-assisted writing instruction. If we trace the history of computer-assisted writing instruction from its early days—say, the 1980s—to the present, we see that writing instructors have greatly modified the ways in which they use the computer as an instructional tool. Most of the theory and the methods described by current literature in the field of composing with computers portray classroom settings that are free from charges such as Cuban's loss of "social relationships" and Monke's loss of our search for "truth" and "great ideas" and "the discovery of meaning."

So, as we point our prows into the winds of the computers-in-education revolution, we must be wary. We must insist that if the computer is to find a place in our classrooms, it must prove that it merits that place. We must examine the available evidence before determining if, how, and to what extent we will use computers as instructional tools. And each of us will reach his or her own conclusions. Nevertheless, I here offer my own: the computer as an educational tool will never live up to the hype it receives, except in one area, and that area is word processing.

Notes

Chapter 1

1. Lisa Gerrard goes on to point out that in stark contrast to the ideals that we as writing instructors have set forth as shared values, we practice "divisiveness" within our departments. We place theorists on the top and the practical (classroom instruction) on the bottom. She notes that the field of computer-assisted writing instruction, as the new kid on the block, had heretofore been free of such internecine strife; but in recent years, theory-versus-practice squabbles of the department proper have begun to creep into the computer sector. She pleads for a return to sanity before it's too late—the acceptance of both theory and practice on equal footing (28–32).

2. The issue raised here by Sally Tweddle and Phil Moore is particularly relevant at the secondary level. Between ten and fifteen years ago, the literature-centered curriculum took over secondary English classrooms across the nation. Despite the near disappearance in professional journals of references to "literature-based instruction," the foothold remains secure. In my own experience, attempting to maintain a literature-based classroom while simultaneously maintaining a student-centered classroom—in the sense of using student-generated texts as the instructional core—is a formidable task. It is possible to devote some time to literature-based instruction and some time to student-centered instruction in alternating time blocks, but to do both simultaneously is impossible. I propose offering literature and writing as two separate classes.

Chapter 2

1. The tendency for those who write with computers to obsess about local-level revision while still in the initial drafting stage—a tendency that I cast in a negative light—has at least one defender. Takayoshi claims that computer-assisted writing "makes dramatically visible the fluid and recursive nature of writing by dissolving segments of writing processes into one seamless flow of prose" (246). Before computers, the recursive nature of composition was a mental construct that one had to comprehend in the abstract; but with computers, this "unconscious mental processing becomes more visible" (247).

2. As I compiled the research for this book, I grew continually more surprised by the mass of journal articles questioning the efficacy of using computers to write or to teach writing. I sense a possibly strained attempt to play devil's advocate, as if an article supporting writing with computers would be scorned as being overly obvious, whereas an article questioning writing with computers is automatically invested with the genius of taking a novel stance. I can't help but wonder if the authors of any of the anticomputer papers I have read—other than Wendell Berry—seriously consider abandoning their computers and returning to pen and paper.

Chapter 3

1. My own introduction to having students write on computers began around 1990. At that time, I was teaching a class titled English Tutorial, a kind of remedial course. Also at that time, our Maclab consisted of only twenty computers. Because there were only twenty computers, the Maclab rarely got used. There weren't enough computers for every student to have one—except in my case. My English Tutorial classes all consisted of fewer than twenty students; as a result, I had free rein in the Maclab. I could take my classes in for a round of word processing anytime I pleased. Today, however, things have changed. The Maclab now consists of over thirty-five computers, a large enough number to accommodate most of the classes on campus. Gone are many of the little SE30 computers that originally populated the Maclab; the lab is now a fifty-fifty mixture of those SE30s that remain and the larger Power Macs that have been added. Now that our Maclab has been so much improved, the administration has decided to meddle. It has converted the Maclab from a "teacher sign-up" system to a mandatory scheduling system. To guarantee that all ninth graders will be introduced to the Maclab, all ninth-grade English teachers are scheduled into the lab for seven consecutive days. By the time the last group of ninth graders completes its orientation, it is May. The purpose of scheduling the ninth graders into the Maclab is to encourage them to use the lab in succeeding years; the result, however, guarantees that no non–ninth grader has an opportunity to use the lab. With my class set of DreamWriters, I am immune from such examples of administrative brilliance.

Chapter 4

1. Here's something to consider: Richard Jewell claims that part of the "maleness" of computers is inherent in their physical arrangement. Computers are most commonly placed in rows, and "row designs turn computer users into lone hackers in the mold of traditional male individualism, and such computer use, while not invalid in itself, can lead us to limit traditionally more female community and conversation" (55). So, if we want to take that extra step in repairing the existing gender inequality, we might consider rearranging our computers.

Chapter 5

1. The exercises described in this chapter assume the use of Microsoft Word. This is not to say, however, that the instructions wouldn't work in other programs as well.

2. Two other rules for constructing sentence modeling exercises are (1) require that the content of the modeled sentences be far removed from the content of the originals and (2) in the case of certain key words, allow students to choose any word *except* the word that appears in the original. In the case of the Kidder sentence, the subordinate clause should not begin with the word *after*; the participial phrase should not begin with *collecting*. Students who are able to form a subordinate clause or a participial phrase that begins differently from the

original are demonstrating that they do indeed know how to form such constructions; students who must rely on the words of the original author are demonstrating the contrary.

Afterword

1. For those interested in reading some cautionary literature on the dangers of placing computers in our schools, two excellent titles include the scholarly *Let Them Eat Data* by C. A. Bowers and the more conversational *High-Tech Heretic* by Clifford Stoll.

Works Cited

Aaron, Jane E. *The Little, Brown Essential Handbook for Writers.* 3rd ed. New York: Longman, 2000.

Beals, Timothy J. "Between Teachers and Computers: Does Text-Checking Software Really Improve Student Writing?" *English Journal* 87.1 (1998): 67–72.

Berry, Wendell. "Why I Am Not Going to Buy a Computer." *What Are People For?* San Francisco: North Point, 1990. 170–77.

Bowers, C. A. *Let Them Eat Data: How Computers Affect Education, Cultural Diversity, and the Prospects of Ecological Sustainability.* Athens: U of Georgia P, 2000.

Chandler, Daniel. "Who Needs Suspended Inscription?" *Computers and Composition* 11 (1994): 191–201.

Christensen, Francis. "A Generative Rhetoric of the Sentence." *Rhetoric and Composition: A Sourcebook for Teachers and Writers.* 3rd ed. Ed. Richard L. Graves. Portsmouth, NH: Boynton/Cook, 1990. 191–99.

Collier, Richard, and Clifford Werier. "When Computer Writers Compose by Hand." *Computers and Composition* 12 (1995): 47–59.

Crafton, Robert E. "Promises, Promises: Computer-Assisted Revision and Basic Writers." *Computers and Composition* 13 (1996): 317–26.

Cuban, Larry. Foreword. *Teaching with Technology: Creating Student-Centered Classrooms.* Ed. Judith Haymore Sandholtz, Cathy Ringstaff, and David C. Dwyer. New York: Teachers College, 1997.

———. "Unless Teachers Get Involved, Wiring Schools Just Enriches Computer Makers." *Los Angeles Times* 10 Aug. 1997: M1+.

DeWitt, Scott Lloyd. "The Current Nature of Hypertext Research in Computers and Composition Studies: An Historical Perspective." *Computers and Composition* 13 (1996): 69–84.

Dowling, Carolyn. "Word Processing and the Ongoing Difficulty of Writing." *Computers and Composition* 11 (1994): 227–35.

Fader, Daniel. *The New Hooked on Books.* New York: Berkley, 1976.

Ferganchick-Neufang, Julia. "Who Is in Power? Student-to-Teacher Harassment from the Traditional Classroom to Virtual Reality." *ACE Journal* 1.2 (1997): 8–26.

Gerrard, Lisa. "Computers and Composition: Rethinking Our Values." *Computers and Composition* 10.2 (1993): 23–34.

Gray, James. "Sentence Modeling." *Theory and Practice in the Teaching of Composition: Processing, Distancing, and Modeling.* Ed. Miles Myers and James Gray. Urbana, IL: NCTE, 1983. 185–202.

Gruber, Sibylle. "Computers in the Classroom: A Process Report." *ACE Journal* 1.2 (1997): 27–32.

Hackett, Joseph. "Poetry with Graphic Highlights." *The English Classroom in the Computer Age: Thirty Lesson Plans.* Ed. William Wresch. Urbana, IL: NCTE, 1991. 49–53.

Halio, Marcia Peoples. "Multimedia Narration: Constructing Possible Worlds." *Computers and Composition* 13 (1996): 343–52.

Hamilton, Joan. "'Song of Myself': A Class Poem." *The English Classroom in the Computer Age: Thirty Lessons Plans.* Ed. William Wresch. Urbana, IL: NCTE, 1991. 66–73.

Hawisher, Gail E. "Research Update: Writing and Word Processing." *Computers and Composition* 5.2 (1988): 7–20.

Heilker, Paul. "Revision Worship and the Computer as Audience." *Computers and Composition* 9.3 (1992): 59–69.

Henderson, Kathy. *The Market Guide for Young Writers: Where and How to Sell What You Write.* 5th ed. Cincinnati: Writer's Digest, 1996.

Heyn, John. "Using Computers to Write Fiction." *The English Classroom in the Computer Age: Thirty Lessons Plans.* Ed. William Wresch. Urbana, IL: NCTE, 1991. 32–34.

Hirsch, E. D. Jr. *The Schools We Need and Why We Don't Have Them.* New York: Doubleday, 1996.

Huffstutter, P. J. "Apple No Longer the Teacher's Pet." *Los Angeles Times* 15 Mar. 1998: D1+.

Jewell, Richard. "Overcoming Classroom Design: Group Writing in Computer Classrooms." *ACE Journal* 1.2 (1997): 52–59.

Jody, Marilyn, and Marianne Saccardi. *Computer Conversations: Readers and Books Online.* Urbana, IL: NCTE, 1996.

Joram, Elana, et al. "The Effects of Revising with a Word Processor on Written Composition." *Research in the Teaching of English* 26 (1992): 167–93.

Kalmbach, James. "From Liquid Paper to Typewriters: Some Historical Perspectives on Technology in the Classroom." *Computers and Composition* 13 (1996): 57–68.

Kantrov, Ilene. "Keeping Promises and Avoiding Pitfalls: Where Teaching Needs to Augment Word Processing." *Computers and Composition* 8.2 (1991): 63–77.

Klonoski, Edward. "Using the Eyes of the PC to Teach Revision." *Computers and Composition* 11 (1994): 71–78.

Loewen, James W. *Lies Across America: What Our Historic Sites Get Wrong.* New York: New, 1999.

Marcus, Stephen. "Invisible Writing with a Computer: New Sources and Resources." *The English Classroom in the Computer Age: Thirty Lessons Plans.* Ed. William Wresch. Urbana, IL: NCTE, 1991. 9–13.

McGarvey, Jack. "Writing a Wrong." *Teacher Magazine* Oct.1997: 52.

Milone, Michael N. Jr. "Staff Development Success Stories." *Technology & Learning* 18.7 (1998): 44–52.

Mitchell, Diana. "Fifty Alternatives to the Book Report." *English Journal* 87 (1998): 92–95.

Monke, Lowell. "The Web and the Plow." *Teacher Magazine* Oct. 1997: 30–34.

———. "Web of Deceit." *Teacher Magazine* Jan. 1998: 42–43.

Monroe, Rick. *Writing and Thinking with Computers: A Practical and Progressive Approach.* Urbana, IL: NCTE, 1993.

Morics, Catherine. "Autobiographical Newspaper." *The English Classroom in the Computer Age: Thirty Lessons Plans.* Ed. William Wresch. Urbana, IL: NCTE, 1991. 109–12.

Neumann, Thomas. "The Mini-Dictionary." *The English Classroom in the Computer Age: Thirty Lessons Plans.* Ed. William Wresch. Urbana, IL: NCTE, 1991. 14–16.

Oppenheimer, Todd. "The Computer Delusion." *Atlantic Monthly* July 1997: 45–62.

Owston, Ronald D., Sharon Murphy, and Herbert H. Wideman. "The Effects of Word Processing on Students' Writing Quality and Revision Strategies." *Research in the Teaching of English* 26 (1992): 249–76.

Peckham, Irvin. "If It Ain't Broke, Why Fix It? Disruptive and Constructive Computer-Mediated Response Group Practices." *Computers and Composition* 13 (1996): 327–39.

Pennington, Martha C. "Modeling the Student Writer's Acquisition of Word Processing Skills: The Interaction of Computer, Writing, and Language Media." *Computers and Composition* 10.4 (1993): 59–79.

Roblyer, M. D. "The Constructivist/Objectivist Debate: Implications for Instructional Technology Research." *Learning and Leading with Technology* 24.2 (1996): 12–16.

Rodrigues, Dawn, and Raymond Rodrigues. "How Word Processing Is Changing Our Teaching: New Technologies, New Approaches, New Challenges." *Computers and Composition* 7.1 (1989): 13–25.

Rohan, Liz. "A Kinder, Simpler Technologically Rooted Pedagogy: Writing Instruction on the Word Processor." *ACE Journal* 1.1 (1997): 20–23.

Ruenzel, David. "Is This the Future of Education in America?" *Teacher Magazine* Jan. 1997: 24–29.

Sabik, Cindy Meyer. "Teaching More, Talking Less: Engaged Pedagogy and Writing Fluency in the Electronic Classroom." *ACE Journal* 1.2 (1997): 45–51.

Sandholtz, Judith Haymore, Cathy Ringstaff, and David C. Dwyer. *Teaching with Technology: Creating Student-Centered Classrooms.* New York: Teachers College, 1997.

Sands, Peter. "From Real Time to Writer's Time: Setting and Reinforcing Goals by Sequencing Assignments and Technology in the First-Year Writing Class." *ACE Journal* 1.2 (1997): 33–38.

Schenkenberg, Mary. "Modeling the Literary Paper." *The English Classroom in the Computer Age: Thirty Lessons Plans.* Ed. William Wresch. Urbana, IL: NCTE, 1991. 3–5.

Schipke, Rae C. "Using Computer Journals to Teach Critical-Thinking Skills and the Writing Process." *The English Classroom in the Computer Age: Thirty Lessons Plans.* Ed. William Wresch. Urbana, IL: NCTE, 1991. 84–94.

Sharples, Mike. "Computer Support for the Rhythms of Writing." *Computers and Composition* 11 (1994): 217–26.

Skeele, Rosemary W. "Technology and Pedagogy: A Professional Approach to Curricular Change in English and Language Arts Education." *ACE Journal* 1.2 (1997): 39–44.

Stoll, Clifford. *High-Tech Heretic: Why Computers Don't Belong in the Classroom and Other Reflections by a Computer Contrarian.* New York: Doubleday, 1999.

Strong, William. *Creative Approaches to Sentence Combining.* Urbana, IL: ERIC/ NCTE, 1986.

———. *Practicing Sentence Options.* New York: Random, 1984.

Takayoshi, Pamela. "The Shape of Electronic Writing: Evaluating and Assessing Computer-Assisted Writing Processes and Products." *Computers and Composition* 13 (1996): 245–57.

Traubitz, Nancy. "A Semester of Action Research: Reinventing My English Teaching through Technology." *English Journal* 87.1 (1998): 73–77.

Trimble, Deborah. "A Manual for Parents." *The English Classroom in the Computer Age: Thirty Lessons Plans.* Ed. William Wresch. Urbana, IL: NCTE, 1991. 54–58.

Tweddle, Sally, and Phil Moore. "English under Pressure: Back to Basics?" *Computers and Composition* 11 (1994): 283–92.

Williams, Debbie J. "Teaching with Technology or the Technology of Teaching: Reconstructing Authority in the Classroom." *ACE Journal* 1.1 (1997): 41–49.

Wolfe, Edward W., et al. "A Study of Word Processing Experience and Its Effects on Student Essay Writing." *Journal of Educational Computing Research* 14 (1996): 269–83.

Wolk, Ronald A. "Techno Utopia?" *Teacher Magazine* Jan. 1997: 3.

Worman, Dwight. "Creation of a Book of Student Writing." *The English Classroom in the Computer Age: Thirty Lessons Plans.* Ed. William Wresch. Urbana, IL: NCTE, 1991. 45–48.

Wresch, William, ed. *The Computer in Composition Instruction: A Writer's Tool.* Urbana, IL: NCTE, 1984.

Zehr, Mary Ann. "Cybergirls." *Teacher Magazine* Mar. 1998: 14–16.

Author

Dave Moeller earned his master's degree in rhetoric and composition from California State University, Northridge. He teaches both high school and junior college English; on the high school level, he has taught for nineteen years. Moeller currently teaches in the William S. Hart Union High School District in Santa Clarita, California.

This book was typeset in Palatino and Helvetica by Electronic Imaging.
Typefaces used on the cover were ITC Benguiat Gothic Medium and Commercial Script.
The book was printed on 60-lb. Williamsburg Offset by Versa Press.